Praise for *Yesterday's Soldier*

"*Yesterday's Soldier* is a Vietnam War memoir of a different flavor. Packed into this tidy book is the story of a young man's coming of age in troubled times. The author, after five years of studying for the priesthood in a religious seminary, leaves and is quickly exposed to the Draft. He chooses to enlist rather than be drafted, and proceeds through the Army's infantry training cycle of weapons and war tactics, which clash with his years of prayer.

During his attendance at the Army's Infantry Officer Candidate School he makes a moral decision: He will wear the uniform and serve anywhere, but in a non-combat role. That decision to be a noncombatant puts him at odds with the Army, his family and his Church.

The story is of his transformation from infantryman to conscientious objector and his experiences in Vietnam. He shares his joys and trials along the way, is definitely worth reading."
— **Mathew Brennan**, Vietnam combat veteran and author
  of *Brennan's War, Flashing Saber: Three Years in
  Vietnam, Broken Helmet* and *Headhunters*

"Keating describes his war and its effect on him in clean detail. His words are personable, yet direct, and bring you right in to his experience. Skills like his are invaluable, so that we may revisit these important experiences in history."
— **Amber Telford,** Firefighter EMT and US Marine combat
  veteran of Iraq

"Tom Keating writes with courage and honesty. Not an easy task when you write about things that you don't want to write about. Wars never end in the mind of those who fight in them. And those around them who witnessed it."
  — **Roxana Von Kraus**, Director, AGAPE Writing Workshop for Veterans, Woods College at Boston College

"A young, patriotic student who has been studying the priesthood in a Catholic seminary for five years leaves to become an army infantry officer in Vietnam. No, this isn't the plot to the next Hollywood Blockbuster, this is Tom Keating's life. The belief in his God and his country inspired him to enlist in the US Army during wartime, but his faith and his ideals caused him to struggle to become a non-combatant conscientious objector. *Yesterday's Soldier* is his story of serving in the same combat theater as all the other military men and women.

Keating uses real language to tell a very accessible story that will put you in his boots. His words show how the US and Vietnam were worlds apart while having underlying similarities. War, religion, and morality are always in the background of his tales, but they move to the surface every once in a while. His memories show a need for understanding others different than us, and our country needs more of these stories today than ever before."
  — **Sean Davis**, Iraq Combat Veteran, author of *The Wax Bullet War, Chronicles of a Soldier & Artist*

Yesterday's Soldier

A PASSAGE FROM PRAYER
TO THE VIETNAM WAR

Tom Keating

Yesterday's Soldier

By Tom Keating
Published by Stratford Publishing

Copyright ©2019 Tom Keating

ISBN 9781705530498
Library of Congress Control Number 2019917956

Author photo by Kathleen Keating.
Jacket design and formatting by Christa's Creative.

This book is dedicated to all
who object to waging war and do
the hard work of waging peace.

Yesterday's
Soldier

"Peace is something you have or do not have. If you are yourself at peace, then there is a least some peace in the world."

– Thomas Merton

Prologue

I was excited and a little scared as my Dad and Uncle John dropped me off at the seminary in North Easton, Massachusetts in the fall of 1963. I'd graduated from high school in June, and was entering the seminary of the Congregation of Holy Cross as a postulant to begin what was called "formation years" before being ordained.

I grew up in the post-World War II suburb of Stratford, Connecticut, the middle child of my parents, Alice and Thomas Keating. I had four siblings: two older sisters, Sally and Kathleen, a younger brother Dan, and a baby sister, Alice.

We were raised Roman Catholic, and attended church every week and on Holy Days. My parents gave us all Catholic education in elementary and high school. I served as an altar boy for six years in our parish church, Our Lady of Peace. Each year the Pastor would dress up the altar boys in fancy Vatican-type cassocks and capes, and have a professional photographer take full color pictures of us as the parish Christmas gift to our parents.

I grew up outside of the city of Bridgeport, and attended public schools till the sixth grade, then my folks sent me to Blessed Sacrament School run by the Dominican Sisters, a bus ride away in Bridgeport. My parents wanted me to pass the entrance exam for the newly constructed Catholic high school in the diocese.

Notre Dame High School in Bridgeport was one of the largest private Catholic schools in the East. Eleven hundred boys and the same number of girls arrived daily to a huge sprawling set of buildings located just outside the city limits. I was taught by young priests from the Congregation of Holy Cross. The girls, in a separate wing of the campus, were taught by the Sisters of Notre Dame De Namur.

The Holy Cross Fathers were well known for their educational prowess—after all they had founded the University of Notre Dame in Indiana. I was a so-so student, good at English, bad at math, a member of the drama club, and I sang with the glee club, but was cut from the football team for being too slow. I did join the debate society where I met and made friends with the smarter, gifted students. I was also on the school's swim team as a third-string breast stroke swimmer and equipment manager.

I was impressed by the priests, my teachers. They were good, and I told my parents in my junior year of high school that I wanted to be like them, a teacher and priest. They were pleased to think that their son was going to be a priest. I applied to the seminary during my senior year, and raised my grades to get accepted—and I was.

The seminary, my new home, was a building dominated by a large chapel and bell tower topped by a stainless-steel cross. It was located across from some hay fields by the campus of the college, Stonehill, which was created by the Congregation of Holy Cross in 1948.

The plan for ordination was to study at the college my freshman year, then living, praying and working on a dairy farm at the

Novitiate the next year in Bennington, Vermont. The Novitiate was where one learned to live a religious life, the Rule of Saint Benedict, prayer, meditation, and how to live in a community. It was at the end of that year that one professed the three vows of poverty, chastity and obedience, and wore the cassock, small cape and cincture.

The Novitiate I attended started with twenty-seven candidates, but the grueling process of living like a monk decimated the number. Many friends, some from my high school, who were postulants with me, left because of the stress. It was difficult seeing my friends leave, and made me wonder if I could stay with the harsh discipline myself. That winter in the low hills of Bennington was especially cold, which added to the stress of Novitiate life.

I surprised myself by being one of the twelve who knelt and took the vows on a fine July day in Vermont. When we returned from Vermont in 1965, our second year of college began, and we studied philosophy and theology for the next four years as professed members of the Congregation of Holy Cross.

My day in the seminary started by rising at 5:30 AM each day for prayer and meditation, followed by Mass. After Mass, we ate a small breakfast in the refectory before heading over to classes at the college. I lived with rules of silence (no speaking), Spartan meals, limited visits from families, strict obedience to Father Superior. Each week "Chapter" were held by Father Superior, where one confessed one's "sins" publicly in front of the whole community.

All of us attended the college courses in groups, wearing our

Roman collars, small capes, and cinctured black cassocks. We sat in the back of the classrooms and refrained from talking to the students, especially the coeds. When classes were finished, we walked back to the seminary building located about a quarter-mile from the main campus. Friendships in the community were discouraged, though I had my friends from high school that were also seminarians: Mike, Dan, Jim, and Ted. We made it through the novitiate together, shared family news, and helped each other with the daily pressures of seminary life, the discipline of the rules of religious community life, the pressure to excel in studies, the family separation, and the continual supervision by the seminary staff.

However, changes to that daily life in the seminary came with the Second Vatican Council and its decrees designed to bring the Church into the 20th century. The liturgy, Mass, the daily prayers, were now in English, fish on Fridays was no longer mandatory, the altar was turned to face the congregation. Cassocks and Roman collars were no longer mandatory dress. These changes were all designed to reach out to the people.

Our Chapter meetings became "T-group" therapy sessions. A T-group is a form of group training where participants learn about themselves through their interaction with each other. They use feedback, problem solving, and role play to gain insights into themselves and others.

These and other changes came during my junior year in college, and the seminary life changed as well. The rigid rules of monastic life were partially lifted, and that allowed me to embrace the reform movement and the ideal of being "Christ's Witness" to the college's students. This disturbed Father

Superior and his staff. They were definitely not in favor of the liberal direction that I embraced, but I was not alone. Some other seminarians followed this liberal direction, too.

Struggling to live a holy life, I watched others leave the seminary, some close friends. It was painful to say goodbye to them as they left, one after another. Of the twenty-seven in my freshman group of postulants, and after five years, only five of us remained. My friends from Bridgeport began to leave the seminary, too, which was extremely upsetting to me. First it was Ted, then Dan, and finally Mike and Jim, whom I had been very close with. It set me adrift, and disrupted my junior year and my religious life. It was noticed by others, especially Father Superior. I was late to prayers, sullen at times, and distant from others.

I threw myself into participation in college activities, worked on the college literary magazine, the college yearbook and the film society, and even helped to organize student anti-war demonstrations. I worked for the Massachusetts primary campaign for Senator Eugene McCarthy on campus, and assisted a small anti-Vietnam War activist group of students. This meant talking with coeds at these activities.

I was looking forward to being sent to Notre Dame University for theology studies and then ordination. I had finally made the Dean's list academically, and my activities on campus with the college newspaper and yearbook were in line with the new attitude in the Church—going where the people are, being a witness to the Lord among them. Near the end of my senior year, I was called into Father Superior's office to receive my assignment to theology studies at Notre Dame University.

It was a shock, then, when he said, "Tom, we don't think you have a true vocation, and we will not send you to theology. You have what is known as a 'temporary vocation.'"

He then read off a litany of reasons for this decision—my grades were not stellar, in spite of my recent Dean's list success. I lacked focus on the spiritual aspect of religious life, distracted by the activities I pursued at the college. My time spent on the campus was time not spent with the community. Of course, it was also not proper for me to be too friendly with the women I worked with at the college. (I had co-signed a student loan application for one, even though I had no money as a seminarian.) I was shaken and hurt and confused. Father Superior had one more thing to say that would really change my life.

"Tom," he said. "We are required by law to notify your local draft board immediately of the change in your status from IV-D, studying for the ministry, to I-A, available for military service. We have to send the letter before you leave here after graduation."

Just like that, my life changed. I was not going to be a priest. I could be sent to a country 10,000 miles away, and could be carrying a rifle, walking in rice paddies and jungle. It was 1968, the bloodiest year of the Vietnam War. I was angry, confused, scared. I got up and left his office. I called my Dad, who came up to drive me back to our home in Connecticut. I had a bachelor's degree in philosophy and a I-A draft classification, a prime target for the draft.

CHAPTER 1

Decisions

I left Holy Cross Seminary right after graduation and faced the draft and the age-old question "What do I do now with my life?" I couldn't afford to go to graduate school, and I didn't want to live at home forever, so I had to find work.

I went to my friend Lou, who owned a drive-in fast food restaurant in the pre-McDonald's era, and was able to work for him slinging hamburgers and hot dogs. That gave me some income, and I was able to pay for gas and drive my dad's car. The summer of 1968 was tumultuous. Robert F. Kennedy and Martin Luther King Jr. had been assassinated; and the Democratic National Convention turned ugly as protesters fought the police in the streets on Chicago. My Dad and I watched the television broadcast of the demonstrations and saw the excessive use of police force on the protesters, and we both were shocked. It was a shared moment between his generation and mine. The Vietnam War was not going well, as the North Vietnamese offensive called TET had killed and wounded many US forces.

Meanwhile, I tried to start a career for myself. I went to interviews all over the area. My interview with the local IBM office was a typical example of what happened. After a long interview with IBM in their Bridgeport office, I was asked to take an aptitude test. The results came back a few days later, and I was called back by the interviewer to discuss the results.

I scored very well, he said. I had an aptitude for computers and a good general education. He said IBM would be happy to hire me for their training program after I completed my military obligation. There was no avoiding military service. My best chance of avoiding being sent to Vietnam was to enlist in either the Navy, Air Force, National Guard, or Army Reserve. The Marines was definitely out of the question, as they were heavily involved in the war.

However, I found that there were no openings in the local National Guard units or Army Reserves. While I was in the seminary, guys had run toward both of them to avoid the Army and Vietnam. My dad told me to talk to our cousin, who was a recruiter for the Army, to see what he could do for me. The first thing my cousin said was frightening—my town draft board had my name up near the top for notice of Selective Service. I was newly eligible since leaving Holy Cross Seminary.

Cousin John and I went over my options, like joining the Navy, or the Air Force for three or four years with a better chance of avoiding the war. Three or four more years in another organization seemed too long to me. The Army had a two-year contract, the same as being drafted, and if you enlisted, you could choose your job, but you had to volunteer, or enlist. I thought this was a better option. It would be a shorter time in the military, and being a college graduate, I had a better chance of being assigned a role in the service not directly tied to Vietnam service.

My cousin also told me something I didn't know. He told me that as an enlisted soldier I would be designated Regular Army, not a draftee, and that would grant me unseen privileges during my time in service. Regular Army, or "RA" soldiers would get promoted quicker, better job assignments, better chances of leave, weekend passes, and other advantageous things. I followed his advice and signed the enlistment papers.

So, in the summer of 1968 I learned I was to report to New Haven for induction in October. Till then, I had time to relax. My college friends were all getting married, beginning their lives. I travelled to friends' weddings—Hope and Troy's, Jim and Kathy's—and enjoyed sharing their happiness.

I worked for Lou through September. It was an election year, Nixon vs. Humphrey, and Humphrey came to Stratford to speak at the Lycoming AVCO plant, where they built engines for the Army's Huey and Cobra helicopters.

Nixon was promising to end US direct combat involvement in the Vietnam War, while Humphrey supported sending more troops there. The Democratic Party was deeply divided over the issue of the war, and Humphrey was seen as a war hawk, while other democrats like Gene McCarthy opposed the war. The country was also divided by those opposing strategies.

The AVCO plant was located right next to Lou's drive-in. I had never been to a political rally so I strolled over to see what it was all about. It was September, late in the campaign and everyone had a hard time getting excited. Chubby Checkers, the singer known for his "Twist" songs, was the entertainment for the rally. I can't remember Humphrey's speech, but the rally ended with the Democrats' famous theme, "Happy Days are Here Again."

Lou sold a lot of hamburgers and hot dogs that day.

CHAPTER 2

Basic Combat Training, Fort Dix

The Armed Forces Entrance Examination Station in New Haven was busy the day I arrived, October 25, 1968. I had a small gym bag containing a change of underwear, and one dollar in my wallet, per instructions. The dollar would be for my regulation hair cut when I started Basic Combat Training. The room where I took my oath of service held about seventy-five recruits. We all swore to uphold the constitution, and so on.

When that finished, a Marine Gunnery Sergeant walked in and told us to line up, tall to small. We did as he ordered, and he went down the line, tapping guys on the shoulder. When he finished, he said, "All those who I tapped, take one step forward." About twelve guys, all big young men, moved.

The Marine Gunnery Sergeant looked at them and said, "Congratulations gentlemen, you are now in the United States Marine Corps. Follow me." The rest of us looked at each other with relief. Everyone knew that the Marines were pretty much heavily engaged in Vietnam.

After our physical exam we were put on buses for the drive to Fort Dix, New Jersey to start training. Arriving in the late afternoon, we were greeting by men in broad-brimmed felt hats screaming for us to get off their bus. The hats looked like those worn by Smoky the Bear in the ads. Basic Combat Training began with our heads shaved ("Give that hardworking barber your dollar!"), and bunks assigned. All while running or being screamed at by the drill sergeants.

They gave us large Army overcoats to wear due to the cold weather, and told us we would be in a week of administrative processing, "zero week" in military terms. After a night's sleep, we were awakened at 5:30 AM, marched to a mess hall for breakfast, and then down to a large building to begin processing into the United States Army.

The staff, all enlisted men and some women, interviewed us, confirmed our identities, administered intelligence tests, had physicians check our lungs and eyes, and sent us to the supply warehouse to draw a basic clothing issue, five pairs of underwear, pants, shirts, gloves, socks, two pairs of boots, a formal dress uniform, and a baseball cap and a field jacket. I remember hearing the song "Those Were the Days" playing on radios on some of the desks. When I hear that today, it brings me back to that large room with all the clerks typing and interviewing confused, bald inductees.

I was assigned to C company, 3rd Training Brigade, located in a collection of World War II type wooden barracks. They were built to last five years in 1940, and were still being used twenty-eight years later. Our days began at 5:30 AM, reveille. We had twenty minutes to shower, shave, and then run to the mess hall in formation to eat breakfast in ten minutes. Drill Sergeant (DS) Hardy and his staff would shout "This ain't no Howard Johnson's, eat your shit and git!"

Everyone had to traverse the monkey bars to enter the mess hall. If you didn't have the upper body strength and fell, you had to repeat the bars till you finished. I was inept at this, and repeated many times. The military draft was in full bloom, and the soldiers who were drafted were designated "US", while Regular Army were always first in line for chow, first in receiving weapons from the Armory, first in the trucks.

Drill Sergeant Hardy was small in stature, wiry, and black. His fatigues were pressed razor-sharp, and the combat medals on his blouse were impressive. Hardy pushed his company hard, harder than other platoons. We ran more, did more push-ups, and generally drilled more. He made us take our M14 rifles apart and put them back together again constantly. We cleaned them spotless each day. Our boots were shined, our lockers organized, our beds made to Army specifications. He was the poster child for Drill Sergeants.

The cold, dry weather of New Jersey that fall turned to snow, but that didn't keep him from pushing his platoon. During the second week of training, in November, I woke up coughing, and was dizzy. I told the Drill Sergeant that I felt ill, and I needed to go to sick call with the medic. He challenged me.

"Private Keating! You ain't sick. You only think you are, but nobody goes on sick call in my platoon, unnerstand?"

I was about to say, "Yes Drill Sergeant!", when I threw up all over him, fainted and fell back against the barracks door. He cleared everyone else out of the barracks and shouted for the other drill sergeant to get the medic. My second week in the Army knocked me on my butt.

CHAPTER 3

Walson Army Hospital

I regained consciousness as I was being hustled into a green Ford Econovan, sitting on the floor with a few other recruits who looked ill, too. The van drove across the base to the Walson Army Hospital, and when the van door opened, there were people there to help us into the emergency room. I was still very dizzy, and the place kind of spun around. Someone felt my forehead, and said, "He's hot." I passed out again.

There isn't a worse time to be in a hospital than during the holiday season, but that November of 1968, I was in the Intensive Care Unit of the Walson Army Hospital. I woke up in a bed, in a dark room. I heard voices, but I didn't understand what they were saying. I thought I was hallucinating. Whenever I opened my eyes, the room spun around. I saw someone in a white coat approach me and stick something in my arm. Everything went black again.

When I opened my eyes again, I was in the dimly-lit room. I still heard the voices, still couldn't understand what they were saying. I closed my eyes. I woke up again and there was a nurse standing over me. She was tall and lean, wearing glasses, with her dark hair pulled back into a ponytail.

"How are you feeling, Private?" she asked. I looked up at her, and noticed that the room was brighter, and it wasn't spinning anymore.

"Okay, I guess. Where am I?" I replied.

"You're in the Intensive Care Unit here at the hospital," she said. "You have pneumonia, and we have been watching you carefully waiting for your fever to break. It came down this morning."

"How long have I been here?" I asked.

"Five days. We put the IV in when you got here, monitored your vitals, and kept our eye on you. The doctor will be here shortly to speak with you. I brought some ice chips for you to sip. Your stomach isn't ready for food or water, yet, but we will see." I took the cup of ice, and put some in my dry mouth. It felt good.

"Thank you," I said.

Later, a doctor did come and speak to me. He told me I had lobar pneumonia, a severe infection in my right lung. The infection had lessened, and they were going to start inhalation therapy and oxygen to clear the lung. I was going to be moved to the respiratory ward later that day.

After he left, I looked around the room, and saw three other beds with patients in them. One of them smiled at me and said, "Ola!"

I said, "What's ola?"

He laughed and told me it was Spanish for hello. He was a member of the Puerto Rican National Guard, and so were the other two guys. They had pneumonia, too, but were not as sick as me. He told me they heard me coughing and wheezing for three days and tried to talk to me in Spanish because they thought I was from Puerto Rico, too. They were the strange voices I heard.

The change in my vital signs allowed them to move me to the respiratory ward, but I got lost in the shuffle, and my family had not been notified that I was sick. They didn't know about my illness for two weeks. It was only when Sergeant Hardy came up to the hospital with my clothing and personal possessions that he found out the Red Cross had screwed up. I was really angry at them for not notifying my family, an anger that never went away.

The respiratory ward was a large room, with beige walls and locked windows at either end. Sixteen beds were placed along the walls, eight on each side. A few chairs faced a large TV hanging from the ceiling at one end of the room. I was wheeled to a bed on the opposite end, near one of the windows overlooking the parade ground. A nurse cautioned me not to go near the window at any time. I found out later that a patient had jumped to his death out a window while on the ward.

A woman wearing a white lab coat introduced herself. She was Lieutenant Johnson, the ward nurse. She told me I would get well by doing what she or the staff told me to do, and that I would take inhalation therapy four times a day. She definitely was in charge.

Every couple of hours a Green Beret soldier who was there for his medical training came by my bed to take my vitals, listen to my lungs with his stethoscope, and adjust my ventilator. He wore his Green Beret insignia and his rank (staff sergeant) on his white lab coat.

The daily routine of treatment and rehabilitation sapped my energy. It was uncomfortable inhaling the medicine-laced steam. I didn't feel any improvement in my lungs. I was discouraged. The treatment caused much discomfort, and the coughing to clear my lungs was constant. My breathing was labored. Nothing was working, I thought.

The television set in the ward was on all day. Watching the commercials full of happy people eating Thanksgiving dinner or shopping for Christmas trees, and buying gifts for each other was depressing. I wanted to be with those people, not stuck in an Army hospital. I became more despondent, snappy, and cranky with the staff. Lieutenant Johnson noticed.

Thanksgiving came, and I was able to eat the "holiday meal," turkey with all the trimmings, that the hospital provided. It felt good to be eating solid food again. I watched football on the large television with the other patients in the ward, and cheered when Harvard "beat" Yale in that infamous 28-28 tie game. My despondency returned, though, the next day. Thanksgiving in a hospital only made me more despondent and angrier.

Later that weekend, Lieutenant Johnson announced that a local entertainer was coming to the ward to sing some Christmas songs for us. After our dinner, the young lady, Carol, arrived in the ward with her guitarist. She sang the standards—"Silent Night," "Joy to the World," and other songs in a clear, crisp voice. The ward grew still, as everyone thought about Christmas and home as she sang.

After about six songs, Lieutenant Johnson brought her over to my bed, and said, "Private Keating needs some holiday cheer."

Carol nodded, and asked, "Can I sing your favorite Christmas song, Private?" she asked. Before I could say anything, she turned to her guitarist and said, "How about 'White Christmas'?" And she began the song.

As she sang, I started to remember past Christmases with my family, listening to Bing Crosby Christmas records, and the happy times we had. My feelings got the best of me, watering my eyes. I started to feel that "Christmassy feeling" like in the TV ads. I smiled at her.

She finished the song and said, "Merry Christmas, Private. Get well soon." Lieutenant Johnson gave me a wink and a smile, then escorted the entertainers over to another ward. I was cheered by the little concert. I think it helped improve my health. My coughing diminished, my lungs and breathing felt better.

The Green Beret nurse continued to visit me every couple of hours to take my vital signs. One day he smiled as he listened to my lungs, and said, "You sound good, Private. You'll be out of here soon." He was right. My infection was being defeated by the massive antibiotic treatment.

I was discharged from the hospital on December 4, and sent home from the Army for twelve days recuperative leave, weak, but on the mend. Because my recuperation leave was in the middle of December, the Army added two more weeks to my leave, as they closed most bases for the holidays. If the Army didn't medically discharge me for my illness, I would not have to report back to Fort Dix till the first week of January 1969. I would be home for Christmas!

I returned to the barracks to pick up my other gear. It was late in the afternoon, and the platoon was ready to graduate from Basic Combat Training. I said goodbye to Sergeant Hardy, and walked over to the bus terminal with my duffel bag as the platoon marched in formation to the gym building for their graduation.

I felt sad that I wasn't with the platoon, but I was sure the Army would medically discharge me after I returned to Fort Dix after the holidays, thus ending my Army "career." I wasn't going to miss being in the Army.

CHAPTER 4

Kill! Kill! Kill!

When I returned to Fort Dix, I was back in Basic Combat Training. Army doctors had declared me fit for duty, thus I had to report to a new Basic Combat Training Company, in the same cluster of old wooden barracks. My orders did state that I should avoid strenuous physical activity for three days. When I stepped off the bus at the Fort Dix Bus Terminal, the frigid air stabbed my weakened lungs like an icicle. I knew my body hadn't healed yet, and I was upset that I was back in Basic Combat Training in the cold winter of New Jersey. January 1969 was one of the coldest and snowiest months on record.

The barracks I was assigned to was in another long, white, wooden two-story building, set in a row with other old wooden barracks built in 1940. A coal stove on each floor barely heated the long narrow room where soldiers slept. Large double-hung windows ran the length of both floors, and were kept open six inches every night to prevent meningitis.

The building had a large open, communal bathroom and a large open shower room on the first floor. Incandescent lights hung from the white rafters, with red "butt cans" placed near red buckets of sand labelled "FIRE." At night, we cleaned and polished our boots under the sickly glow of bare, large yellow light bulbs hanging from the rafters.

My bunk was located on the second floor, a single bunk at the far end of the room. I was the new guy, and the platoon was already in its third week of training as a unit. I was the stranger.

I had my own bunk because I was a late addition to the company. Others in the platoon had to share lockers, and use the bunk beds, but I was alone with my own single bed and locker. Some resented the fact that I had my own space, my own locker, a sliver of personal privacy that they lacked. The platoon was a mix of National Guard members, draftees, and volunteer enlisted like me. With one exception, everyone was from the Eastern United States and mid-South.

The next morning, combat training started. It was a cold, wind-swept day, and white snowflakes parachuted gently down while we ran up and down the barracks road; then came calisthenics. My damaged lungs could barely keep up with the running and physical training. I had to drop out, and it pissed off the others because they had to wait for me in the cold air.

My new drill sergeant, Sergeant Crocker, knew I had been ill, but I had to participate in all the physical activities like the rest of the platoon, regardless of what the doctors said about avoiding strenuous activities, and it was really hard on my weakened lungs.

Adding to my stress and anguish was Dexter, a young, slightly built farm boy from Ohio. He took an instant dislike to me. I think it was because I was the new guy, of course, but also, I had my Boston accent, which sounded foreign to him. I used big college words he hadn't heard before, like "obsessive" ("the Drill Sergeant is obsessive") and "excrement" ("this food tastes like excrement"). New guy indeed.

He made my life miserable. His bunk was near mine on the right side of the bay, and when I was away from my bed and locker, he would sneak over and tear apart my bunk before inspection, or scuff my highly polished boots. These infractions caused me extra kitchen police details, or fire guard duty at midnight. At first, I didn't know who was doing this, but after a few incidents, realized it was him. He was always smirking when the drill sergeant screamed at me for these infractions.

He was encouraged in his vandalism by Larry. Larry was a National Guard soldier in our training platoon. He was the recruit platoon leader, chosen by the drill sergeant because he was tall and big shouldered, like a football linebacker. He resented the fact that I was dropping out on runs, and holding up "his platoon." He was trying to get the award for the "Soldier of the Cycle" given to outstanding recruits in basic training, and my delays reflected poorly on his performance.

Larry was fond of telling all of us that after Basic Combat Training, he was going back home to Albany, New York to be in the National Guard while the rest of us would "get yur asses shot off in 'Nam." I was frustrated by the continual harassment, but I chose to turn the other cheek. After all, I had left the seminary only six months earlier. Peace, prayer and forgiving those who sin against you had been my life for five years.

During our fifth week we finished weapons training and were sent to the rifle range to qualify as infantry riflemen. This time we didn't march, but were transported by large, long-bed truck trailers used to transport horses or other livestock, so our shooting wouldn't be affected by the physical exertion of marching to the range.

Even as the snow fell on that cold windy day, I was able to accurately fire my M14 rifle. I scored high as an expert rifleman, along with a few others in the platoon. The Drill Sergeant rewarded his best riflemen with a weekend pass off the Post. The rest of the platoon, including Larry and Dexter, didn't make expert, so they didn't get passes. I enjoyed a short break from the Army with my family in Connecticut for twenty-four hours.

When I came back and walked up the stairs to the platoon area that Sunday everyone stopped talking, and watched as I walked toward my bunk. It was torn apart, the blankets, sheets and mattress on the floor; my footlocker busted open, and the contents thrown everywhere. Dexter stood by his bunk stifling a giggle. I looked across the room at Larry who tried hard not to smile, waiting to see how I would react. The rest of the platoon paused, waiting.

My rage inside me exploded, my face turned bright red. I reached into my wall locker for my bayonet, and ran over to Dexter, tackled him, put my knee on his back, pulled the bayonet from its scabbard, pushed his head down and put the cold steel edge of the bayonet against his neck. I shouted, "If you ever fuck with me or my stuff again, Dexter, I am going to kill you. So help me God! Right here, right now. Got it?"

Nobody moved. I held the blade against Dexter's warm neck just like they taught us: "What is the spirit of the bayonet? Kill! Kill! Kill!" we screamed during training on the bayonet course.

Dexter didn't move. The barracks were funeral quiet. Blind with rage, time had stopped for me. After a scary pause, and with a shaky voice, Dexter said, "Yeah."

I pulled the bayonet away and let go of him and stared over at Larry. He looked away, and I walked back to my bunk, my heart pounding, and put the bayonet in its scabbard and back in the locker. My hands trembled as I started straightening things out, and I shivered from the cold air that hit my sweat-soaked shirt. The room remained quiet for a minute, then someone said "Okay," and people went back to their business, shining boots and brass buckles.

My hands stopped shaking after a few minutes, and my body twitched as I cooled down. I could not believe what I had done. Oh my god, I was going to kill that kid! I shivered again and realized that Basic Combat Training was working: I had learned how to kill. Five years of God, prayer, love, and kindness was gone. The Army had done its job. I cleaned up the mess and got ready for the next day.

Larry and Dexter didn't bother me again. We finished our training three weeks later. The National Guard troops went home, including Larry, who left with two black eyes and a split lip from a midnight beatdown from the draftees just before graduation. They had grown tired of his cracks about them being cannon fodder. The rest of the Platoon received their orders to various training facilities in the Army. I was assigned to Fort Jackson, South Carolina, for Infantry Advanced Individual Training (AIT).

Eight months later, after more training and a brief stay at the Infantry Officers Candidate School (OCS), I was standing in a line with other soldiers, at the telephone exchange center at McGuire Air Force Base, in New Jersey.

I was waiting to call home before boarding my flight to Vietnam. The place was packed with soldiers dressed in new green jungle fatigues, green baseball caps, and nylon combat boots. Everyone was waiting in lines to use the phones and speak to family, wives, or girlfriends.

I glanced over to the next line, and there was Dexter. The kid I almost killed with a bayonet to stop his harassment of me back in Basic Combat Training. He saw me and his eyes got big, then he smiled and said, "Hey, Keating!"

"Hey, Dexter," I replied, "how you doing?"

He nodded, "Okay. I'm a telephone lineman, you know, climb the pole, fix the wires. I'll have a good job when I get back home. You?"

"Admin specialist, you know, clerk typist," I said. Dexter nodded again as his line shuffled forward. I thought— "Climbing telephone poles in a war zone, Jesus!" He nodded again, as his line shuffled forward.

"Good luck," he said, moving with the line.

"Good luck to you too, Dexter," I said. As he shuffled away, I remembered how he made my life miserable back at Fort Dix during Basic Combat Training, and how I nearly cut his head off. My anger for what he did to me in Basic Combat Training was replaced with a sudden compassion for this young, slightly built farm boy who was going to war. For the first time since the seminary, I found myself praying for someone. Silently I prayed to St. Michael, patron saint of soldiers, "Dear St. Michael, Protect him and bring him back home."

It felt good praying for someone else.

CHAPTER 5

The Green Comet Diner and the Weekend Pass

A weekend pass was treasured, especially for those of us who lived in the Northeast, because we could be home for a good part of that twenty-four hours, if we planned it right. The process was pretty simple—if I left at noon on a Saturday, I could make it back by duty time on Sunday.

Change into my Class A uniform, with the tan collared shirt, the black tie, the green jacket and pants, wearing my little used, but spit-shined black dress shoes instead of combat boots. One yellow chevron stripe on my sleeve, signifying my rank as a Private. One ribbon over my left breast, the National Defense Ribbon. Report to the orderly room for the 24-hour weekend pass as Sergeant Crook or Sergeant Hawkins, whoever was on duty as charge of quarters, checked my uniform, and issued the pass when the clock showed 1200 hours. Walk over to the main roadway to catch a Post taxi. It usually fit six or seven guys in one cab. Fares were a quarter each, and we all told the driver to "take us to the bus station."

At the tan brick bus station, we became part of a large mob of soldiers waiting for buses, either to Philadelphia, or New York City. I was headed to New York. I stood in another line to purchase my round-trip for the Port Authority Terminal there.

When the bus arrived, soldiers piled in. I sat down in the first seat I could find, and fell asleep during the two-hour ride. In Basic Combat Training, you never got enough sleep, so you slept when and where you could. Other guys would smoke and talk about what they were going to do or see in the city.

The bus stopped at Newark Airport, and the commotion of guys exiting the bus always woke me from my nap. Guys would get off to catch a plane, or just go home. It would be another forty-five minutes, going through the Lincoln Tunnel, until the bus pulled in at the Port Authority Terminal.

I left the bus and took the escalator up to the main level, trying to find the quickest bus to Bridgeport, Connecticut and home. The terminal walls were covered with advertisement posters, symbols of a civilian life that was alien to me: posters for new cars, new movies, new Japanese motor scooters. I found a phone booth and called home to let them know I was coming. My brother Dan said he would be waiting for me at the Bridgeport bus station. If I was lucky, the Greyhound bus would be there and I could just make it. More often I had to wait an hour for the Trailways bus, which usually left at 3:10 PM, arriving in Bridgeport at 4:45 PM.

To kill time, I would go up the escalator to the noisy bowling alley and bar on the second level and order a beer. Sometimes a gay man would approach me and offer to buy a beer for me. The man would comment on how nice I looked in the uniform, and how about a quickie in the men's room? Soldiers in the platoon who came through the Terminal had warned us about these guys. I wasn't surprised. I didn't feel threatened. I always declined the invitation, but accepted the beer.

The Trailways bus left exactly on time as it headed out of the terminal, onto the Hudson River parkway, through Spanish Harlem and past Columbia University before connecting to Interstate 95.

I saw another soldier on the bus, really just a kid, a recent graduate of the paratrooper school, going home on rest leave with a broken arm. Blond, blue-eyed, and probably seventeen-years old, he told me he couldn't wait to kill the Viet Cong. I was shocked at his eagerness to kill, not realizing that I was going through the same indoctrination. When the Trailways bus drove onto I-95, my anticipation intensified. The bus went through the Greenwich toll, then stopped in the Stamford bus station.

The blond paratrooper got off there, and the bus went back onto Interstate 95 to Norwalk, then to Fairfield. I knew I was almost home when I could see through the window the roadside sign for the Green Comet Diner. The sign was below the Interstate, on the Black Rock Turnpike, high above the diner so I could see it on the Interstate. It depicted a large green neon comet tail trailing big green letters that flashed "THE GREEN COMET DINER" as we passed. The bus turned off Interstate 95, turned onto Water Street in downtown Bridgeport, and pulled into the recently built yellow brick bus terminal facility. I was home on my weekend pass.

Dan was there waiting at the bus station in his Volkswagen (VW) Beetle with the flower power decals all over it. Dan was eighteen, and in full hippie fashion. He was wearing bell-bottom slacks, a fringed jacket, and he sported long red hair and mustache. He looked like George Custer. I hopped in the VW and we headed out of Bridgeport, back on Interstate 95 for the quick ride to Lordship, my home on the coast of Long Island Sound.

Lordship is a small town on a peninsula that jutted out into the Sound. Single-family homes built after World War II were spread all over the town. We had our own elementary schools, a volunteer fire department, three or four churches, and we were close to a small former military airport now used by private air services.

My house was a small Cape Cod style house near the water. Darkness came early in the winter, but the warm yellow glow of the lights in the large "picture window" of our house spilled out to welcome me home as Dan turned into our driveway.

It was around 5:30 PM, and my mom and dad greeted me with hugs and kisses. I had arrived just in time for dinner, and mom would have my favorite meal on the stove, her spaghetti with meatballs. We ate in our small dining room, and I talked about my week at Fort Dix, keeping out the nasty events like the barracks fights or the foul-mouthed shouts of the drill sergeants, so my folks wouldn't be concerned. I ate two or three helpings of the juicy meatballs, because Army food never tasted like home-cooked food. After dinner, we all gathered in the larger living room to watch the television, which sat in a corner.

There was a couch against one wall, under a large mirror, and three soft chairs arranged around the room. The venetian blinds were lowered at the large picture window facing the street. Dan would head out to be with his friends, but my sisters usually joined us.

In 1969, there were only three national television channels to watch, plus a few local channels that broadcast local sports or old black and white movies.We watched "The Jackie Gleason Show," from Miami Beach, followed by my mom's favorite, "The Lawrence Welk Show," and then the crème de la crème, "Hollywood Palace," a variety show with dancers, singers and comedians. The program was usually hosted by Bing Crosby or other big-time Hollywood stars like Dean Martin or Sid Caesar. It showcased many musical guests like Frank Sinatra, The Rolling Stones, Tony Bennett, Liberace and comedians like George Burns, Jack Benny or Bob Newhart.

I stayed up late watching the Saturday movie on the local station, usually a black and white horror film like *It Came from Outer Space* or *Frankenstein* with Boris Karloff. Once in a while, a good western would be on. When Dan came home around that time, we'd watch the movie and drink beer together. I would share my Army experiences with him. I told him about the brutality, the awesome killing power of the weapons we fired, my incident with Dexter.

The next morning, Sunday, we all attended Mass at Our Lady of Peace Parish where I had served as altar boy. Friends and neighbors, seeing me in uniform, came over to say hello, and show their concern. They all wanted to know if I was going to Vietnam. Some also had sons also in the military, a few in Vietnam.

After Mass was over, we would pile into Dad's blue Rambler and head to the Duchess Diner in Stratford for breakfast. The Duchess was a classic modern diner, all glass and aluminum, with Formica tables and juke box stations right at the table. The eggs, bacon and toast servings spilled over the plates, and coffee cups were never empty. We talked about everything: my sister Sally attending nursing school, Kathy's job as an X-ray technician, Dan's VW, Dad's job.

When we got back to the house, I'd read the Sunday papers, and maybe watch the first quarter of the New York Giants football game with my Dad and Dan, then get ready for the trip back to Fort Dix. My Mom made me a lunch for the trip back. Dan would drive me back to the Bridgeport bus terminal around 2:00 PM to catch the bus back to the Port Authority Terminal, where I could catch the Trailways back to Fort Dix.

We had to be back by 1800 hours, or 6:00 PM. I usually made it to the Company area by 5:30 PM. The trip back took about four hours door-to-door, weather permitting. I was heading back to Basic Combat Training, the Army life, and probably Vietnam, and wondered, what the hell had I gotten myself into?

CHAPTER 6

Infantry School, Fort Jackson

My orders for infantry school had been delayed, and Jim, one of the other soldiers whose orders had also been delayed, hung out with me around our barracks at Fort Dix, waiting for our orders. We even used the company day room (recreation room), which had a color TV, pool table, soda machine—things we never saw during Basic Combat Training. Every training company had a company day room, and I'm sure none of the trainees ever set foot in one.

The orders arrived at last, and the Drill Sergeant put me in charge of travel, because I was a college guy and a candidate for Officer's School. He handed me a ticket voucher on the Sunshine Limited, the famous New York to Miami train, for twenty-five tickets.

When Jim and I arrived at Penn Station for the trip, the clerk asked me where the other twenty-three soldiers were. I didn't know.

We had club car seats on the train. There were many old folks going to Florida who were curious when Jim and I came into the club car wearing our Army dress uniforms. One woman asked me, "Are you Marines? My husband was a Marine. We met on the train when he was on leave in 1942."

"No, ma'am," I said. "We are in the US Army, going to Fort Jackson down in South Carolina."

The train arrived in Washington, and Jim and I had to switch trains. The local train to Columbia, South Carolina would be leaving the next day, so we stayed near the train station overnight at a local YMCA. Again, there were twenty-five reservations on the voucher, but only the two of us. We continued on the train the next day, through Maryland, North Carolina and arrived in South Carolina, and Fort Jackson, located outside the city of Columbia, the state capital.

An Army bus was waiting for twenty-five of us, of course. I went to C-6-3, Infantry AIT (Advanced Individual Training), Jim to vehicle maintenance training. My barracks were in new brick buildings with squad bays, new single beds, and air conditioning. I was assigned to learn the skills of being an infantryman. The 11-week program was designed to teach soldiers how to use the weapons the Army employed in Vietnam.

These weapons included the new M16 rifle, the M60 machine gun, .45 caliber pistol, grenades, explosives, and Claymore mines. We also learned military radio procedures, first aid, helicopter procedures, even rappelling from helicopters. I learned how to work with a fire team, practicing the small unit tactics of attack, defense, and air assault.

Our company training officers were not combat experienced, except for Lieutenant Joseph, who had just returned from combat in Vietnam. The officers were in training, too and it showed during our maneuvers. They kept getting the platoon ambushed, or lost.

Lieutenant Joseph bragged about how he drank rice paddy water to get sick and be relieved from duty, and sent home. I could not believe it when he told us that. It made us all wonder how terrible Vietnam was if an officer would do that to get out of there. Great message for us trainees.

Another training cadre would suddenly begin to weep as he tried to tell us how to avoid booby traps. He would apologize to us for his tears, telling us he survived enemy attacks, but had to bury his buddies. And that had fucked him up, seeing his friends die so horribly in battle. He said it made him become a Catholic. That got my attention. It was less than a year since I left the Catholic seminary. I was already a Catholic and wondered what I would convert to if I got fucked up over there. The war was part of our daily discussion now, as we all learned the battle arts. These stories did not inspire us.

During the training at Fort Jackson, I scored high with expert ratings on the M16 automatic rifle, which replaced the M14 rifle I knew so well in Basic Combat Training. My lungs still were a problem, but at least I had no Dexter in the platoon.

Our sergeants were all recent graduates of the Non-Commissioned Officers (NCO) school at Fort Benning, where soldiers were trained to be squad sergeants. My platoon leader, Sergeant Potter, reminded me of Andy Griffith in the movie *No Time for Sergeants*. He was always smiling, even after getting us ambushed or lost on training maneuvers. He was just happy to be in the Army and be a sergeant. He didn't much like us northern boys, and always found a way to screw around with us, especially college graduates. We were always assigned to kitchen duty, cleaning pots and pans, or harassed about our boot shine, minor stuff like that. There were three of us in my squad: me, Eniner and Kroft, both from the Midwest, and both national guardsmen who would go back to Indiana after training.

We worked hard on our weapons training, because most of us knew where we were going after the training completed. The Vietnam War. We rappelled from static platforms, learned to eat snakes and bugs, how to remove leeches, all to prepare us for jungle training.

The weapon that impressed me, no, scared me the most was the Browning M2 50 caliber machine gun. It was a frightening weapon, considered a heavy weapon, and not because it weighed a lot. It fired a cartridge that was almost six inches long, one half inch in diameter, and its effective range, the distance it could be aimed to a target with accuracy, was almost one mile.

When it was my turn to fire the damn thing, I was reluctant. It was just an industrial killing machine, and it frightened me. I cringed at the thought of what one of those bullets would do to a human. The range officer saw my hesitation and sneered, "Whatsamatter, Keating, ain't you a killer?"

"Sir, no sir!" I replied, and took my position, and fired ten rounds at the target. The noise was incredible. When I stopped firing, my hands still shook, more from fear than the weapon vibration. I was very happy to let the next soldier sit behind the M2.

CHAPTER 7

Whiskey and Graduation

Near the end of our training, a few of us took one last weekend pass. Soldiers on weekend passes were expected to be well behaved. Fort Jackson had special "Courtesy Patrols" of MPs that roamed downtown Columbia looking for any trouble-makers among us. They could and would stop us in the street and ask for our Department of Defense armed forces identity card and our paper company pass, and tell us to shine our shoes, or get a haircut.

When Kroft, Eniner and I went into town for that last weekend pass, we checked out at 1200 hours from the training company, and we jumped on the bus to take us to town, along with other soldiers.

The first thing we did when we arrived in town was locate the state liquor store to buy a cheap bottle or two of whiskey. The clerk tried to give us some crap about selling liquor to "Yankees" because of our Northern accents, but we were all twenty-one years old, so he had to sell us the booze.

We bought Rebel Yell Bourbon, only sold (then) "south of the Mason Dixon line." Its label featured a Confederate Soldier on horseback holding a saber high, with the phrase "Celebrating the great victory at Chickamauga"—definitely a Southern brew. It was smooth, smoky and cheap.

We took our booze with us into the local movie house to watch the new Clint Eastwood and Richard Burton film *Where Eagles Dare*, a war movie. I guess we were in the mood for explosions and guns, even though it was movie make-believe. We sat there drinking and laughing at the battles by Eastwood and the good guys, who never missed a shot, and were never wounded.

The bourbon put a buzz on us, and when we left the theater, we were careful to avoid the Courtesy Patrols. We returned to our motel room that was reserved for all of us by one of our southern squad members. Soldiers with northern accents at that time were refused reservations often—they didn't like us. Of course, the room, once reserved, would soon be filled with ten of us sleeping on the floor, the bed, and one of us in the bathtub. We drank some more, and then headed out to see what was going on in town.

We headed down main street and noticed a United Services Organization (USO) sign on the sidewalk outside a hotel. The USO was a service organization of civilians that tried to make life easier for soldiers, sort of like the Red Cross, without the emergency. The sign read "USO Dance Party All GIs Welcomed." We couldn't resist.

A local band was playing tunes from the fifties as the three of us walked into the hotel ballroom, and there were GIs dancing with young ladies. Still buzzed from the bourbon, we spotted our company sergeant across the room talking with young women who were dressed as if they were at their high school prom.

A young woman came over and welcomed us. Pointing to a table full of cookies and bottles of soda, she told us we could have some soft drinks and cookies, and if we wanted to dance with the "young ladies," we needed to buy dance tickets over at another table, ten cents each. The money was to go to the operation of the USO. We nodded and headed for the ticket table.

I bought a dollar's worth, ten tickets, but Kroft and Eniner were stingy; they bought just five tickets. We walked around the ballroom, approached a couple of the young women, showed them our tickets, and proceeded to dance with our partners. My partner, a dark-haired slim girl, being polite, asked me where I was from. I said "Boston, Massachusetts." She stiffened up. "You're a Yankee!" she said.

"Yes, ma'am, and proud of it," I replied. She stopped talking, and her dancing became labored, so we stopped. I gave her the rest of my tickets, nodded over to my buddies, who had similar reactions with their dance partners, and we left.

The eleven weeks of AIT came to an end in April of 1969. I earned the military classification of 11B10, rifleman. My infantry skills were superb—expert rifleman with both the M14 and M16. Expert machine gunner, one who could take apart the M60 machine gun, put it together and skip the rounds into the target. I maxed all the skills tests. However, the pneumonia I contracted in New Jersey during Basic Combat Training had scarred my lungs, and they had not recovered.

I had to run an eight-minute mile in combat boots and fatigues to graduate from infantry school, and I made it with five seconds to spare, thanks to the drill sergeant exhorting me to finish the last quarter mile. I was now a trained killer.

One year earlier, I was living the semi-monastic life of daily prayers and lofty spiritual idea of "love thy neighbor" as a seminarian in North Easton, Massachusetts, and now I was an accomplished infantryman. Back then I never thought about killing, or how to load a machine gun, or how to use a tourniquet. Then, it was all prayers and study. Now it was how to survive and kill in battle.

CHAPTER 8

Baseball and the Drunk

Because I was a college graduate, I was assigned to go to Infantry Officer Candidate School (OCS) at Fort Benning, Georgia as part of my enlistment agreement.

It seemed once again that my orders to report to Fort Benning hadn't arrived when everyone else got theirs, so I was put on work details for a couple more days. Meanwhile, my payroll and personnel records had already been forwarded to Fort Benning. When my orders did arrive, I could not draw any funds for the trip. All I had was an Army bus ticket, a meal voucher for $2.00, and $1.50 in my pocket.

I spent the next twelve hours on a bus, stopping at every small town in South Carolina and Georgia, during which I spent the cash and voucher on snacks, soda and cigarettes. There was a final stop in Atlanta for a bus change, and a ninety-minute layover. Out of cigarettes and hungry, I walked out of the bus terminal, my duffle slung over my shoulder, stretching my legs and trying to distract myself from hunger pangs.

I walked about a block from the bus station, near the baseball stadium, home of the Atlanta Braves baseball team. It was a hot and muggy night. I heard a man sort of singing, turned and saw a guy sitting down in an alley entrance, his legs spread out, his clothes rumpled, and a cluster of dollar bills in his right hand. He was drunk.

34

He was bathed in the light of nearby street light. The guy looked middle-aged, and was wrapped in a dirty, wrinkled tan raincoat. He was sitting near some trash cans, singing about Billy Joe jumping off a bridge.

As I got closer, I could that his face was ruddy and unshaven. My stomach reminded me that I hadn't had a meal since we stopped in Augusta, Georgia hours earlier. The cash he was clutching could get me some dinner.

I thought, "He's begging to be robbed. This will be easy, just take a few of his bucks, walk away and get a hamburger and a coke. If he gives me any trouble, my hand to hand combat training will do the trick." I kept walking toward him, he kept singing. Cheers from the fans at the baseball stadium down the street competed with his singing. No one else was around. I looked around one more time as I got close, about six feet from him, almost standing over him. Then I stopped abruptly.

Something wasn't right. I don't know what it was, but I thought "Don't do this!" So, I stopped, looked around again, as he looked up to me with a drunken smile. I turned away, hitching my duffle higher on my shoulder and headed back to the bus station.

I took about five steps when his singing stopped. I looked back at the drunk, but he was gone. That fast. Just gone. Spooked by his disappearance, I walked faster to the bus station. Maybe it was a police decoy, or a guy who wanted to rob me?

Either way, I was angry and ashamed about what I almost did—rolling a drunk for money. Five and one-half years of daily prayers and lofty sermons of "God is Love" in my seminary life were gone. That life, that belief in the goodness of people, had been pretty much stomped on by seven months in the Army. Damn! There must have been some left, though, which may be what stopped me from beating this guy and robbing him. I never thought I would ever beat up or steal from another person. I wasn't brought up that way. I was taught to be a peacemaker, and be like Jesus. "Blessed are the Peacemakers for they shall be called the children of God."

No one would call me a child of God anymore. I was now a product of the United States Army Infantry and its training.

CHAPTER 9

Officer Candidate School

At Fort Benning, OCS candidates ran everywhere, all the time. Run to class, run to the firing range, run to meals, run to bed. I was physically and psychologically exhausted every day. Run, do pushups, get yelled at by the tactical officers who were trying to weed the weak from the strong.

My lungs continued to betray me as I dropped out of runs and paid for that failure, crawling up and down "Hamburger Hill," a small but steep rocky hill near our barracks, as punishment for my failures. The company First Sergeant noticed I was not holding my own, physically. My physical impairment was obvious.

I was frustrated by my physical health, and the constant punishment it brought. I vowed to stick it out as long as I was able. When we weren't running around, we were learning tactics and weapons in classrooms. I wanted to be as good as the other candidates, but my lungs still were not fully healed.

Weekends they let up on the discipline somewhat. Candidates were given tasks to complete around the company area. My duty one Sunday was watering the small patch of grass in front of the barracks. I connected the hose and began spraying the lawn. It was about 1400 hours. Without warning, tears flooded my eyes. Startled, I straightened up, but the tears kept flowing. They would not stop.

Now I became frightened, confused. Was I cracking up? I
didn't know what was happening. It struck me then, what was
going on. After eight months of Army life learning to shoot, stab
or blow up people without any qualms, I realized that I could
not kill another human. What was I thinking, joining the Army?
I trained to be a priest, not just a priest, but a priest in an elite
religious order that helped people with prayers and spiritual support. I had to stop being a part of the killing machine called the
Army, or I would really crack up.

I thought back to incidents that should have told me what I
really believed: My revulsion and shame after I assaulted
Dexter with the bayonet in Basic Combat Training; the
hesitation and fear I showed when firing the Browning M2
50 caliber machine gun during infantry training at Fort Jackson.
The range officer had sneered at me: "Whatsamatter,
Keating, ain't you a killer?" He was right. I was not a
killer. I couldn't even beat up a drunk for food.

I finished watering the patch of lawn in front of the barracks, and
went to the First Sergeant's office to tell him. I said, "I've made
a mistake, I can't kill anyone, I can't lead anyone else to do that
either. What can I do?"

He listened as I explained to him about my five years in religious
life, my pneumonia in Basic Combat Training, how I realized
I could not justify bearing arms, or killing another. He was
sympathetic, and expressed dismay that the Army hadn't
medically discharged me for my severe pneumonia and weak
lungs back in December.

He then discussed my next steps, but warned me that because I had trained and qualified as expert in all infantry weapons, the Army might reject my application because I never objected to using weapons. The Army could punish me if I refused to serve. I could be court martialed and sent to Fort Leavenworth and hard labor. The First Sergeant said that the Army would question my sincerity and might see my request as a way to avoid going to Vietnam. Many soldiers were trying to avoid service in the war in 1969, as the war became more controversial to many Americans.

Anti-war demonstrations were getting larger, television news broadcast the horrors of the fighting every night. Young men burned their draft cards, and refused to report for induction. Some fled to Canada for refuge. During this time of upheaval, many soldiers had doubts about the reasons for fighting 10,000 miles away in a country nobody had heard of, and they didn't want to die there. The applications for conscientious objectors had increased.

Faced with this, the Defense Department had to set a policy to limit the number of conscientious objectors serving in the Armed Forces. Weapons training without objection would elicit a negative response to any application.

His instructions were clear. First, I had to volunteer to leave the Officer Candidate School. Then, I had to write an application for status change to conscientious objector.

He repeated his warning to me that if I wanted to be discharged from the Army as a conscientious objector it would be a hard sell as I had not objected to any weapons training. Of course, at the time I was trying to learn them I had not realized I was turning into a killer. Applying for discharge from the Army as a conscientious objector, he said, meant the Army would probably reject my application and I could be punished by being heavily fined and/or sent to prison.

He suggested that if I declared in my statement that I would continue to serve my enlistment as a noncombatant, perhaps as a combat medic, or chaplain's assistant, that might satisfy the Army. After all, I was Regular Army, not a draftee. That was in my favor.

I decided to listen to his advice and apply for conscientious objector status while continuing to serve, "I-A-O" in military terms. First, I had to write a resignation letter to the Officers Candidate School. After completing the official Army form, and attaching my resignation statement, I handed in my application and request form to the commanding officer of the 51st Company, and left the Officers Candidate School. The process for filing the change in status travels through the chain of command, from the OCS commander to the base commander, to the Pentagon and then back to the OCS commander.

The process was supposed to take anywhere from four to eight weeks. For the second time in less than a year, my future had changed, first from being a priest, and now from being an Army officer. The first change was not my choosing, the second change was my choice. I was ready to face the consequences for that choice.

CHAPTER 10

Casual Company

After leaving the Officers Candidate Brigade, I was assigned to the 1st Casual Company. Casual Company was a military administrative unit for men in transition, waiting for either orders for overseas assignment (Vietnam) or a change of their status (discharge, reassignment, etc.). Men in the unit were called "casuals" and considered a labor pool on the Post, performing work details like Post Engineers (i.e., garbage men), kitchen work, unloading or loading trucks, or light construction out on the firing ranges.

Casuals lived in a World War II wooden barracks, located near the airborne jump school towers, where jump school students still shouted "Geronimo!" Yes, *Geronimo*, as they jumped from the practice platforms. Each morning, around 6:00 AM, along with the other casuals, I huddled silently in the small parade ground for roll call formation in the dark—two lines of men in green fatigues, baseball caps tilted low on our heads, the darkness obscuring our faces, with a cool breeze chilling the air slightly as we stood waiting for our names to be called for attendance. After breakfast, we formed up again for work detail assignments.

Although we were considered "in transit," we were still in the Army. Daily roll calls, formations, and work details assignments were the order of the day. The work details included being a garbage man, collecting garbage twice a day.

Part of that job required that someone clean out the kitchen grease traps in many mess halls on the Post.

There was "Post Policing," which was picking up litter around the base all day in the Georgia heat, armed with a large canvas bag and a short stick with a nail point for stabbing the trash. And on the weekends, both Saturday and Sunday, repairing sandbag bunkers out on the firing ranges.

As a former OCS candidate and conscientious objector applicant, I became a target for the Army's "Treatment," which was sort of an unofficial policy of generally making my life difficult until I broke and withdrew my application. The Army wanted to "break me" and force me to change my mind about applying as a noncombatant. They had spent a lot of money and time on training me how to kill, and they wanted their investment to pay off. This systemic abuse was made famous in the novel *From Here to Eternity*. It occurred at the company level, by sergeants with the tacit approval and encouragement of officers. As a result, I was usually assigned to Post Engineers during the week, and sandbag repair on weekends. That was part of the "Treatment."

That first week it didn't take long for the "Treatment" to escalate. "Shakedowns" were surprise inspections of personal property that the company officer and sergeant would perform, usually in training companies. They could and did literally shake down bunks, lockers and footlockers for contraband like marijuana, weapons, whiskey, pornography and seditious material.

I was caught in a supposedly random shakedown inspection, right after breakfast as we gathered in the barracks before heading out to our daily work details. The company commander and his sergeant announced the surprise inspection, ordering us all to attention at our bunks.

Then they walked straight to me and my bunk. It was obvious that I had been singled out, marked as a trouble-maker for applying for conscientious objector status. Everyone stood at attention next to their bunk as the lieutenant stopped at my bunk, opened my wall locker that held my extra fatigues and boots, and saw that everything was regulation. Not a problem. He pulled apart my neatly made bunk, throwing the mattress and sheets on the floor, but there was nothing there.

Then he dumped my footlocker and all its neatly arranged contents on the floor: underwear, socks, shoe polish kit, and three paperback books, all of which were allowed by regulation.

The Lieutenant picked up the first book. It was titled *Kiss Kiss, Bang Bang*, a collection of film reviews by Pauline Kael, then the country's most popular movie critic. The second paperback was *The National Advisory Commission on Civil Disorders*, also known as *The Kerner Report*, about the 1967 race riots in the United States. The last book was a cheesy Matt Helm spy novel. The Lieutenant read the title of the Kael book and went ballistic.

"Kiss Kiss, Bang Bang! A skin book! This Private has pornography, Sergeant! Put him on report!" he shouted, throwing the book down. The sergeant wrote down my name. I was standing at attention so I could not speak.

Referring to T*he Kerner Report*, he said, "…and he's got a communist book here, too." He threw that on the floor, too. He ignored Matt Helm.

"This is an Article 15 violation, a VY-OO-LAY-SHUN, Private!" he shouted at me. "Have this Private report to my office for an Article 15 hearing at 1700 hours! Sergeant, police up this contraband!" He turned away and left the barracks. I was in trouble my first week in Casual Company. Article 15 violations could lead to jail, confinement to barracks, demotion and pay garnishment. I was, as they say, fucked.

The sergeant looked at me, smiled as he bent to pick up the books, and said, "You're on Post Engineers tomorrow and every day until I say different, Private Keating." He left. The other soldiers in the barracks just shook their head at my bad luck. Some wanted to know where to buy that "skin book." After cleaning up my space, I spent the rest of the day confined to barracks restriction, cleaning the latrine, polishing the floors, filling the fire buckets with sand. The Army doesn't like it when you interrupt their plans to make you a killer.

That evening at precisely 1700 hours, wearing my starched fatigues and shined boots, I reported to the company commander's office. I walked in, saluted and came to attention.
"Private Keating reporting, as ordered, sir!"

Across from me and behind his desk sat the lieutenant, the sergeant, and, to my surprise, the battalion chaplain, a major. The contraband books were on the desk.

"Keating," he spoke after returning my salute, "we all have looked at your books, and this kiss kiss book, it's movie reviews. So, we can't charge you with pornography." He picked up *The Kerner Report*.

"This here report on the riots is a government published document, so we can't charge you with being a communist for having it in your possession," he drawled. He nodded toward the chaplain. "The chaplain has advised me that I can't charge you, so all charges are dismissed. That is all."

"Yes, sir!" I said, picking up the books. I saluted him, turned smartly and left.

The next morning, after breakfast, I hopped on the garbage truck as a Post Engineer, the sergeant being a man of his word. Innocent or not, I had disrupted his daily schedule, and I was gonna pay for that.

The worst part of the detail was cleaning out the big grease traps outside each of the Post's kitchens. The grease was bad enough, but the smell of old chicken, beef, eggs, and whatever else was in the trap was overpowering. It was hot, crummy work. But I didn't really mind. It was better than going to jail for reading Pauline Kael.

CHAPTER 11

The Process

I wrote my full appeal for conscientious objection in the Fort Benning Post Library, using the *Encyclopedia Britannica* and microfilm issues of the *New York Times*. I was able to pull quotes from a couple of Papal Encyclicals, including Pope John XXIII's *Pacem in Terris*, which fortunately for me, was published in full in the *New York Times*. The Pope clearly abandoned the Church doctrine of "Just War," and I quoted him in my document. I wrote letters to my former teachers and spiritual advisors in the seminary for their support. They responded with strong recommendations that I be granted noncombat status. I did not ask Father Superior for his recommendation.

After I filed the appeal, I wrote to my parents to tell them what I was doing. My parents were upset. They didn't understand why I would leave Officers Candidate School, why I would cause trouble. They were concerned about my mental state. I learned just how upset they were when they contacted the Fort Benning Senior Chaplain to counsel me.

The Senior Chaplain, a Lieutenant Colonel and a Roman Catholic priest, pulled me out of morning formation to talk to me about my application. We talked outside the barracks, near where his vehicle was parked. I didn't know what he wanted till he said, "Your family has contacted me. They are very upset about what you are doing. They want you to reconsider." I felt punched in the stomach. My family was betraying me, and was on the side of the Army! I was sad, and I'd never felt so lonely. It was my struggle for sanity and my soul, and they wanted me to surrender both to the military. My sadness quickly turned to anger. The hell with them! I thought, as the chaplain continued to speak.

He explained to me that as a Roman Catholic, I could not claim conscientious objector status because of the Church's "Just War Doctrine." Apparently, he had not read the Papal Encyclical, *Pacem In Terris*, where the Pope had rejected that doctrine, but I didn't correct him. He insisted that the doctrine ensured that the Vietnam War is morally justifiable against what is evil, and the Church declared communism evil. Therefore, war against the Vietnamese communists is justified, and members of the Catholic Church had to serve in defeating evil. The communists were the anti-Christ, and as a Roman Catholic, I must defend the Faith. I listened to him politely, said "yes sir" a lot. I finally told him I could not in good conscience withdraw my appeal. He was disappointed, and left. My anger with my family strengthened. I felt they had betrayed me, not supporting me, by taking sides with the Army and the Church. I had to fight alone.

The OCS Brigade chaplain, whom I saw at the hearing, also had to review my application. He was a Southern Baptist minister, and he called me to his office where we talked for about an hour. His office was small and windowless, located in the battalion office building. He looked like a kindly uncle, bald, with some gray hair over his ears, wearing wire-rimmed glasses.

We sat fact to face, as I answered all his questions. He queried me about my seminary experience, how long I had been there, what my beliefs were, how I came to this decision. He was surprised that I still could speak some Latin and Greek.

He was impressed that I quoted Pope John XXIII's Encyclical in my defense. My voice trembled when I told him about my weeping while watering the grass, and my sudden realization that I could not kill. We talked for an hour.

At the end of the interview, to my surprise, he told he believed I was sincere in my belief and he would support my claim for conscientious objection. I was relieved. I could not believe that a Southern Baptist Minister embraced my cause while the church I grew up in deserted me.

Another part of the process for applying for noncombatant status in the Army was a visit to the base psychiatrist to ensure that objecting to killing people for my country was not a sign of insanity. Shades of *Catch-22*, the book by Joseph Heller. I was sent to the base offices, located in large red brick buildings, where I took a series of tests to certify that I was not insane. Each time I visited the psychiatrist, I was asked to state what day it was, where I was, why I was there, did I have a soft spot on my head, and so on. This went on for several weeks, along with a physical exam and blood tests.

Eventually, the appointments to the psychiatrist stopped, and his assistant examiner, a young enlisted soldier, whose name was Stuckey, was assigned to my case. Specialist Stuckey was sympathetic to my appeal, being a graduate of another Catholic liberal arts college, the University of Detroit, in Michigan. He had his own problems with the Army. He said that many men mentally unfit for combat service slipped through the screening process because the Army needed more men in the combat arms. Stuckey arranged to have me meet him each week for "counseling," which gave me a break from work details. His kindness helped me through the stress of the "Treatment" those first weeks.

We would have discussions on the war, politics, literature, and movies, like the recent college graduates we were. Once a week, I felt like a normal person, and I was grateful.

Thirty-seven years later, I found his name on the Internet and sent him a very late thank you letter, and provided my phone number. He called me, and we had a great chat. He was pleased that I sent the letter and happy that I survived the war.

CHAPTER 12

Do Not Fold Staple or Mutilate

Soldiers came and went in the 1st Casual Company, because that was the nature of the holding company—a way station for GIs waiting for a change in duty status or assignment. I became one of the longest residents of the company while the Army decided my case. It was difficult to make friends in such a situation.

After almost six weeks of the "Treatment," it stopped. I guess after all the interviews with chaplains, psychiatrists and Army officials, my sincerity was respected. Stuckey helped, too. He told me to be the model soldier, respectful and "not to be bitching about anything and do what they say." It worked. I started getting better work assignments that were more befitting my college education, like sorting mail, or filing forms at battalion headquarters. One day the company sergeant called me out of the morning formation and told me he had a special assignment for me.

"You know about computers, college boy?" he asked.

"Yes, Sergeant, I do," I said, lying through my teeth. I had once helped a professor in college carry boxes of his IBM punch cards to his car, but that was the extent of my computer experience.

"I got a captain who needs computer help over at building 36. I want you to report to him by 0830 hours. Go change into your best set of fatigues, and shine those boots. Don't fuck this up, Keating. I don't have a lot of computer guys around here."

"No problem, Sergeant," I replied. I didn't know what the hell I got myself into, but I was sure it beat collecting garbage.

I headed over to Building 36, walking slowly in the morning heat. It was located across from the paratrooper training grounds. Soldiers training to be paratroopers were running around the track singing, "I wanna be an airborne ranger, I wanna live a life of danger." I was pretty certain they would get that opportunity real soon.

Building 36 was a long one-story wooden building from World War II, painted white with a tin roof. An olive-green Chevrolet sedan was parked outside.

When I opened the door to the building, cool air from window air conditioners greeted me. I saw two long tables set up, with boxes of papers on one, and long narrow boxes of IBM cards on the other just like the ones I carried for the professor. Folding chairs had been arranged around each table.

The captain, a slim man with blond hair and blue eyes, was standing in the middle of the room, arranging papers and pencils. He was my age, wearing the Army's short-sleeved summer tan uniform.

I walked over to report to him. "Private Keating reporting," I said, as I saluted him.

He returned my salute and said, "Good morning, Private. Thanks for volunteering." He smiled at his joke. I noticed he had scars on both his forearms, as if he threw his arms up to protect his eyes from an explosion. He wore a Purple Heart Ribbon and a Combat Infantry Badge on his uniform. He had been in some combat, for sure.

On his sleeve was the black and yellow patch of the 1st Cavalry Division, the Airmobile Division famous for being in the thick of the fighting. He wore his West Point class ring, shiny and heavy, on his right-hand.

"Our job is to check this raw data," he said, pointed to the piles of paper, "and verify that information on these IBM cards. You can read punch cards?"

I lied again. "Yes, sir," I replied.

"Good! When the rest of the detail gets here, we can start."

The building was air-conditioned so the IBM cards wouldn't get soggy or mushy from the Georgia heat and humidity. Three large window A/C units were humming on the opposite wall, and windows and incandescent light fixtures hanging from the ceiling gave us light to read.

There were plenty of boxes on the tables and I figured this detail was going to last a couple of weeks. No heavy lifting, and in air-conditioning!

Twelve more soldiers, some of them also recently resigned candidates from OCS, arrived and the Captain organized us into two groups, data readers and card matchers.

The data on the sheets was rifle range reports on soldiers' marksmanship on ranges from various bases in the US. The IBM card data had to be matched and verified before being run on the computer. Guys who had been to college and who were OCS dropouts became the IBM card readers. Early on in the detail, someone brought a portable radio to the building for background music as we worked.

One day, the song "Ruby, Don't Take Your Love to Town" came on. In the song, Kenny Rogers sang about a wounded veteran and "a crazy Asian war." I looked up at the Captain for his reaction to the words "crazy Asian war" thinking he would be amused. I was wrong.

The song had triggered something different. He stared out the window, his face hardened as his mind jumped back to the firefight that left its marks on him. His right hand briefly touched his scarred left arm as he stared out that window for almost ten seconds.

He caught himself and looked around to see if anyone noticed. I was the only one who did. I smiled and nodded toward him, as if to say "it's okay," and he kind of half-smiled back. I went back to my IBM cards. No one else had noticed, and I didn't tell anyone about his reaction.

The job did take two weeks to finish, and I helped the Captain load the boxes of IBM cards and data sheets into the trunk of the drab olive-green Chevy.

"Thanks for volunteering, Private Keating," he said with a big smile, repeating his joke.

"You're welcome, sir," I replied as I gave him my best OCS cadet salute. He returned it, got in the Chevy and drove away.

CHAPTER 13

Orange Julius and the Nun

By early May 1969, I had become a model soldier, doing my work details and not causing any trouble, just as Stuckey recommended. The "Treatment" eased off somewhat, and I received my first weekend pass off the Post sometime that month. It gave me a chance to spend time in the city of Columbus, Georgia, away from the Army.

I had my pay packet in my pocket, $88.00, and I put on my one set of civilian clothes, jeans and a short-sleeved polo shirt. I got off the bus downtown on Saturday afternoon and went into a state liquor store and bought a pint of cheap Rebel Yell Bourbon that I had acquired a taste for back at Fort Jackson in South Carolina.

I booked a room at the Ralston Motor Inn, an old hotel in the tired, downtown section of the city, a four-story red brick building that was once a four-star hotel, but now was shabby and worn. It only cost $10 for the night. Perfect.

The desk manager rang for the bellhop to take me to my room on the third floor. The bellhop, a gray-haired old gent, dressed in his red jacket with a gold shoulder tabs, asked me if I wanted any company, and said he could get me either a white or colored girl, $5 bucks for an hour. I said no thanks as the elevator opened to the third floor.

I put the key in the door and went in. My room had a high ceiling in the style of old hotels, with light brown patterned wallpaper. There was a small black and white TV on a low chest of drawers, and a small writing desk with the Gideons Bible atop it, near a large window with venetian blinds and long curtains. A small bathroom was across the room, through a door. I sat on the bed and opened my bottle and took a long sip.

It was my first Saturday afternoon off the base, away from the Army. I was alone. I thought maybe I should take up what the bellhop offered. I was still a virgin, having lived in celibacy in the seminary, and the thought of having a prostitute for sex was tempting, but of course years of religious life and moral rectitude kicked in, so I didn't ring for the bellhop. Knowing me, I probably would have tried to "save" her instead of having sex.

It was nearly dinnertime, and I had spent a total of nineteen bucks, a quarter of my monthly income, for room, bourbon and bus fare. I was hungry, and could not afford the hotel menu, so I left, looking for cheaper eats. As I walked along the street, I saw a sign on an old red brick building that read "The Hidden Door-Beer Available Upstairs."

I went up a flight of wooden stairs, and walked into the bar. In the dim, smoky light, I saw US Army patches and other military items hanging on the walls. Loud country music blared. It wasn't crowded. A couple of older guys with military style haircuts were sitting at the bar and they turned to look at me.

I went up to the bar and asked for a draft beer. The bartender gave me a strange look. He asked to see my armed forces identity card. Every member of the Armed Forces had one.

I showed him mine and he said, "OK, this place is for GIs only, just checking."

The beer was cold, the glass almost clean. I leaned on the bar and turned around to look the place over. The walls were covered with large military unit patches painted on large wood disks. The Confederate stars and bars flag hung over the bar.

The waitresses, all Asian, were attractive in their tight mini-skirts, hip-high boots, beehive hairdos and skimpy halter tops. One of the guys at the bar told me that the "girls" were wives of soldiers, most were Korean, not "Veetmeese." I finished my beer, and nodded for a refill, a bargain at thirty-five cents a glass. The refill was cold, and I drank quickly, and enjoyed watching the waitresses. I thought it was strange that an Army bar in the States had Asian women servers, dressed in sexy outfits. I finished the beer and left the bar, went back down the wood stairs, and out on the street. I was still hungry.

As I walked along a series of brick store fronts, I noticed an Orange Julius sign and headed for it. I remembered Orange Julius from the New York World's Fair in 1964; it was the hit of the Food Pavilion, along with Belgian Waffles. The restaurant was sandwiched between two other storefronts in a large old brick building.

I walked in. It was small and narrow inside. A large bucket of oranges was on the counter and the juice extraction/mix machine was on a stand against the back wall behind the counter. Past the counter was a small eating area, about six or seven small round tables with chairs, where one could eat and drink.

Hot dogs were rolling on the cooker, and bowls of relish and mustard were on the counter near the cash register. The menu on the wall behind the counter also listed hamburgers and Coca Cola, but the best deal was their special—two hot dogs and the orange drink for ninety-nine cents. I went for the special.

The couple behind the counter smiled at me. They both greeted me in what I thought was a German accent. The woman was short, maybe fifty years old, with a slightly bent back, and gray hair. She asked, "Are you hungry, young man?" I said yes, and ordered the two hot dogs special.

"You may sit where you like," she said. I moved to the back and sat at one of the tables, facing the door.

While her husband mixed and whipped the drink on the machine, she sat down with me and asked where I was from since "you don't talk like a local boy." I told her I was from Connecticut, and I was in the Army waiting for orders to go to Vietnam. She shook her head, and looked sad. "It is a terrible war," she said. She told me that she and her husband were from "the Old Country" and came to the US after the Americans liberated their camp. They settled here. Her husband interrupted her story.

"Order ready!" he said.

She got up and picked up a tray with the orange drink, straw and hot dogs, plus a mustard and relish cup. She put it all on the table. There were three hot dogs on the tray.

"I thought the special said two hot dogs?" I said.

The woman said, "Ach! It is mistake, eat anyway, you are too thin!", and gave me a wink and smiled. The hot dogs were tasty and hot, the drink foamy, sweet and orangey. Satisfied that I was eating, she got up and returned back behind the counter.

I finished my feast, went up the counter and put a dollar on the tray. Her husband laughed and made a big deal of ringing up the sale. He handed me the penny change. It was getting dark and I had to leave. I told them I would be back the next time I got a pass, and headed back to the hotel.

When I got to my room, I turned on the black and white TV to watch "The Jackie Gleason Show" on CBS. I used to watch that show with my family back home. Watching the program made me sad and homesick.

I was sitting alone in a cheap hotel room, drinking cheap Rebel Yell whiskey, feeling sorry for myself, and the mess I was in, dreading the thought of whether the Army would send me to jail or Vietnam. Drinking didn't help my mood, and I got more depressed. I thought again to call down for the bellhop and get some company, but instead, I picked up the phone, dialed the outside operator, and called a nun in Boston whom I met at the seminary during a summer course at the college the previous year.

Sister Marilyn lived in a convent in Charlestown, Massachusetts. I called there, reversing the charges, hoping she was there. A woman's voice answered, and asked who was calling. I told her who I was, and that I had to speak with Sister Marilyn. She told me to wait. I was relieved. She was there.

During that summer course we'd became good friends. She wrote me encouraging letters when I left the seminary, and continued writing me when I joined the Army and when I was sick in the hospital. Sister Marilyn picked up the phone, and said "Tom? Are you, all right?"

No," I said. I paused and took a breath, "Marilyn, they're gonna send me to jail or Vietnam! I'm in Georgia, sitting in a hotel alone, drinking whiskey, and I'm scared." My voice cracked.

Silence on the other end, then she began to speak. I really didn't hear what she was saying at first. Just hearing her friendly and gentle voice began to calm me down. She spoke of the power of prayer, faith in God, knowing that Jesus is with me. He has a plan for you, words and ideas I heard and tried to live every day when I was in the seminary. I realized how much I missed that life, how alien my Army life was in contrast. My heart thumped, and my chest heaved.

"Tom? Are you still there?' Sister Marilyn said, "Remember that summer at Stonehill College?" She began to hum a song. It was "Try to Remember" from the show *The Fantasticks*. I smiled as I remembered. During that summer of 1967, we first met as we worked together in a course/workshop session on creativity at Stonehill, where Sister shared the cast album of that show as part of her presentation.

As she softly sang the tune my heart thumped again. I laughed and said, "Yes of course!"

She stopped and said, "Keep the good times in your mind. You'll get through this." For a couple of minutes, I wasn't lonely. I was back in a happy time and place. I wasn't alone.

"Thanks, Marilyn. I gotta go now, this must be costing you guys a fortune."

"Take care, Tom, and remember We will be praying for you. God Bless you."

"Thanks, Marilyn. Goodbye." I hung up. Her voice had brought back to me what I left there in the seminary. I drained the pint of Rebel Yell, shut off the television, and fell asleep with the song playing in my head.

CHAPTER 14

Dream Detail

The routine at 1st Casual Company continued. I was the longest-staying member assigned to the company, having been there for two months. I still got work details, but usually they were more in line with my work for the Computer Captain, paperwork for other jobs, and definitely not as hard as Post Engineers work. I had regular weekend passes issued to me. They became opportunities for me to leave the Post and go in to Columbus for a nice meal and overnight stay at the hotel. I also had my weekly visits to Specialist Stuckey at the psychiatrist office.

One of the most difficult things I had to do was ask my family to send me money, which they did. Eighty-eight dollars a month did not cover the expenses of weekends in town. I called home every once in a while, but I was still angry with them because of the Catholic Chaplain incident.

New faces continued to arrive at 1st Casual Company, and new officers and sergeants arrived, too. The new company sergeant, Johnny Johnson, was a young man with three Sergeant's stripes on his sleeve. He was thin and lanky with a Georgia drawl. Johnson had an easy way about him and he walked like John Wayne, all shoulders and hips. He noticed my good behavior and was happy he didn't have any problems with me.

After morning formation one day, Sergeant Johnson called me

over and said that the Computer Captain had called him and complimented me for the work I did on his project. Johnson then asked me if I could type. You never volunteered in the Army, but something told me to say yes, which I did.

"Good. Change into your best fatigues, shine those boots, and report to 1st Sergeant Howell at Officer Candidate Company 53, up on the hill," Johnson said. "They need a temporary company clerk."

Company clerks were the backbone in the Army, they did all the important paperwork: payroll, attendance, weapons issue, etc. Johnson said it was a long-term assignment, and that it may delay my appeal process, which I figured was okay.

Wearing my fresh fatigues and shined books, I walked over to the Company area, near my former OCS company. I knocked and entered the First Sergeant's office of Staff Sergeant Howell, a large black man.

"Private Keating reporting for detail, First Sergeant," I said, coming to full attention. He welcomed me and asked me to take a seat next to his desk in his small ante office next to the commander's office.

He asked me some questions about my education, and why I was in casual company. I told him about my resignation from OCS and my application for conscientious objector. He told me that when he was in Vietnam, two of his soldiers were Conscientious Objectors, and they did their jobs during combat operations. He had no problems with my application and pointed to the typewriter on the desk.

"Let's see what you can do." He handed me a sheet of paper with some writing on it, and asked me to type it on a blank pre-printed Army Disposition Form. I quickly read the copy, and then set the form in the manual Remington typewriter, checked the margins, and spacing, and ribbon, and began to type as deliberately as if it were one of my college term papers. When I finished, I carefully took the page out of the machine and handed it to him and waited.

He looked it over, and said, "Pretty good. I guess you'll do. You will be my company clerk for a while. I'll call Sergeant Johnson and let him know. You can report here tomorrow at 0730 hours." He said the detail was "for a while." I could not believe it. I finally got it, the Dream Detail! No more lining up in the early morning at 1st Casual for attendance and work assignments. A regular working day schedule, time off on weekends, except for the odd weekend the Company was in the field.

Walking back to the company area, I silently thanked the Computer Captain for this semi-permanent detail. I had achieved nirvana for a casual soldier, a semi-permanent detail!

I worked for Sergeant Howell and his OCS company commander for two months. He had my status changed to 71L, administration specialist, thus assigning me a work specialty. I met the company commander, a Captain who had been awarded the Medal of Honor for his actions in Vietnam. He never complained about my appeal, or my work. I was diligent in making a good impression on him, Staff Sergeant Howell, and the Captain's secretary, Sheri, a civilian employee. I reported for duty there every day, in fresh laundered and starched fatigues, which I paid for myself. I wanted this detail to last as long as it could.

My primary duty was completing the Department of Defense Form 1, the morning report of the Company. It had to be error free, with four carbon copies to be distributed. The form contained the daily headcount, equipment list, weapons list, etc. It usually took an hour or so to do, if I had no distractions. It was a good work detail, and I enjoyed every day of it. I felt my luck was changing after all the harassment I experienced the past few months.

CHAPTER 15

Barracks Buddy

I wanted to share my good fortune about the new detail with Pierce, my buddy in 1st Casual Company. Pierce was a member of the battalion communications permanent staff at headquarters. We met at breakfast in the mess hall one day, early in my appeal process, when I overhead him make a comment about the Mets going to the World Series. We were in the food line and I laughed and told him that the Red Sox would get there first. He laughed in reply. That began our friendship.

Pierce had a mellow voice, always spoke quietly. He had a great smile. Both of us were strangers in a strange land. We were "Damn Yankees" from the North. He was an African-American from Brooklyn, me a red-headed Irishman from New England. We "talked funny" as people said. I had my Boston accent and Pierce had his New York accent. Talk funny indeed.

I was struggling with the Army's decision, battling every day with military hostility to my noncombatant claim. Waiting for the decision was stressful, so having Pierce as a friend was a blessing. It made me feel like I wasn't alone, that I had someone to talk with every day and grumble and bitch to about the Army. We ate dinner together, watched TV afterwards in the USO recreation center ("Laugh-In" was a favorite), and talked about baseball, ("What if Seaver pitched to Yastrzemski?"), and what we would do after the Army.

When I received a weekend pass, after four weeks of weekend assignments, I asked Pierce about going to town together, but he said no because his job kept him busy on weekends. We continued to get together for dinner at the mess hall and to watch TV whenever we could.

My appeal came to an end in mid-July, 1969. I was called out of formation one morning and told to report to the company commander. Sergeant Johnson escorted me to the Captain's office, and I was frightened. I knew the Army had made a decision on my appeal. I could be walking into an arrest by the Military Police, or some other punishment. When we arrived, I entered and saluted.

"Private Keating reporting," I said.

The captain returned my salute, told me to be at ease, and handed me a memo from the Commanding General's Office, US Army Adjutant General. I saw the words I'd struggled to see for four months: "Request Approved."

My noncombatant status had been approved by the Army! I was officially I-A-O, Conscientious Objector status while continuing to serve in the Army. That meant I was not to be assigned a combat role, or issued a weapon the rest of my tour in the Army. My relief was exhilarating. My heart was filled with joy knowing that I didn't have to kill.

The captain dismissed me and as we left his office, Sergeant Johnston told me I was going to be sent to Army Medic school at Fort Sam Houston, Texas for Combat Medic Training. Medics were in short supply in Vietnam, especially those who were attached to combat units. I was going to be trained to save lives, not take lives. That was okay with me. He also told me I would be leaving in a few days. I went over to notify Sergeant Howell, who congratulated me and wished me well at Fort Sam Houston.

However, two days later I was notified by headquarters that because the training was a 16-week course, the Army decided to send me over to Vietnam, designated I-A-O, but without a job specialty while I still had a full year of active duty service. My joy at receiving my new status was diminished a bit, and I wondered where I would be assigned, and what duty I would have in the war. Maybe at a fire base as a clerk, or with a hospital as an orderly, or graves registration attendant somewhere. Pleased but scared of going to war, I went over to the Battalion office and told Pierce my good news. He said, "Yeah, I knew they were gonna do that."

"What? How?" I asked.

His answer shocked me. He told me that he was really an Army Criminal Investigation Division (CID) agent, and had been assigned to investigate me. Apparently, the Army didn't trust me. They thought I was a communist (the shakedown incident?) who would stir up trouble with the other casuals. So, Pierce was assigned to befriend me and make sure I wasn't being a troublemaker. That seemed funny to me because I was too concerned about MY own life to worry about convincing others to declare objection to the war. But this was 1969, colleges were on fire with protestors, and the establishment, the military, the government were all threatened.

Pierce said his job was to be a friend to me and see if I was stirring up anti-war sentiment with the other guys in Casual company. He even had a record of where I went on weekend passes, where I ate, who I talked to, etc. That was why he refused my invitations on weekend passes. He was "working," following me.

In his report to the Criminal Investigation Division he told them I wasn't an agitator, wasn't causing trouble, and was a model soldier. The more he talked, the more upset I became. I was horrified at this betrayal. I thought we were friends, united by love of baseball and being educated guys from the North. I was shocked and pissed off by his deceit, the whole idea of being investigated like a criminal. I turned and walked away.

Later that week I was "out-processing" from Fort Benning, preparing to fly home for twenty days leave before going to Vietnam. Pierce showed up at the barracks to wish me luck. My anger and hurt had by then given way to the joy of heading home. I was still shocked by his deceit, but I thanked him for helping me through my struggle, even if it was under false pretenses. We shook hands.

As he left, he said, with a smile, "Ya know, my Mets are really gonna win the World Series." I laughed once more.

Three months later, while on guard duty in a smelly, hot bunker in Vietnam, I listened on Armed Forces Radio while the Mets won the World Series against the Baltimore Orioles.

CHAPTER 16

Leaving on a Jet Plane

I had about a month of leave before shipping out to Vietnam. Most of it was filled with seeing friends and families, including my friends and their parents, who had been in war, either World War II or Korea. I didn't mention my new noncombatant status because some of them had sons in the Navy and Army, who were probably going to Vietnam.

My family was understandably upset, and my brother Dan, with his long red hair and beard, (he looked like a stoned George Custer) was outwardly cool about me going over there, but I knew he was upset. I convinced Kathy, my girlfriend, to come down for a visit before I left. She and I had met at Stonehill College at a summer conference while I was still in the seminary, and she kept writing to me after I joined the Army.

Kathy was a Cambridge Irish beauty, tall, "dark Irish" with a great sense of humor. She grew up with her mom, a single parent, and played basketball for her high school team in Cambridge, Massachusetts. A graduate of Regis College, she lived in an apartment in Braintree and taught English to middle school kids in the suburbs of Boston. My family loved her from the get-go, and her delicate Boston accent drove them crazy. My brother observed "she talks like a Kennedy."

The last day she stayed with us I took her to the local zoo in Bridgeport. Kathy was wearing a lovely yellow pantsuit, her brown tresses wrapped up in a Hellenic hairdo.

When we returned to my car after lunch at the café near the zoo, I turned on the radio and they were playing "Leaving on a Jet Plane." Kathy looked away. We were just beginning to be close and now I was going to be leaving on a jet plane for Vietnam. I was heading to war and it was going to be tough on her. She left for home the next day, with a huge container of my Mom's spaghetti sauce, and lots of hugs and kisses.

Two days later, after a tearful goodbye from my Mom, Dad drove me to the train station in Bridgeport, on the Friday before Labor Day in 1969. We didn't talk during the drive, and I knew he was upset. When he was my age World War II was raging, and he lost friends in the war while he was at home, deferred from military service because he was an aircraft engineer. A year ago, he thought I was going to Notre Dame to study theology and be ordained a priest. Now, I was heading to McGuire Air Force Base to board a plane to the war in Vietnam.

When we got out of the car, dark clouds were filling the blue sky. I picked up my duffel bag from the back seat. My Dad hugged me and said, "Keep your head down, don't volunteer for anything, and come home." We hugged again, and then I headed to the station.

The train ride to New York went by in a blur. The train was jammed with passengers due to the long weekend. I arrived to a crowded Penn Station and walked over to the Port Authority bus Terminal to catch the bus to Fort Dix, just like I did a year ago.

Two hours later, the bus arrived at the base holding area at McGuire Air Force Base, where I checked in with my travel orders. I exchanged my fatigues for new, green jungle fatigues and boots. My vaccination records, and other paper work, including my standard military will, which the Army notarized, were checked, and the billeting clerk assigned me to an old, dark and dirty wood barracks in the holding area for transportees for Vietnam.

My plane would leave in perhaps two or three days, so I had time on my hands, watching guys come and go. I was reading an old *Esquire* magazine article called "M," which was about an infantry unit in Vietnam. The story was grim and real about Vietnam. Meanwhile, the news was blaring about the death of North Vietnamese leader Ho Chi Minh. Guys were saying, he's dead, now the war is gonna be over, and stuff like that. I was sure it wasn't. Wars don't end like that. I just turned on my small transistor radio and listened to the rock music on WABC radio coming in from New York City.

I went down to the mess hall for supper, then walked over to the recreation building, a brightly lit old airplane hangar full of pinball machines and other types of games. The place was crowded with guys waiting for their plane trip, distracting themselves with pinball games and 3.2 beer (a low alcohol beer). I started playing one of the coin-operated games, called, I think, Genius. Put in your quarter and answer the questions that popped up on the screen. The questions were easy, and if you chose the right answer by punching a button you scored points. Point totals displayed on another part of the screen. The more points, the smarter you were. You could be Dumb, Smart, or Bright, all the way to Genius.

As I advanced through the levels, other guys began to notice. I answered the final tough group of genius questions, and the word "Genius" flashed on the board, and bells rang and the lights flashed. My audience was impressed, and couple of them slapped me on the back. "Boy, you're smart!" one of them said. I smiled back and bathed in the praise, till I heard one guy say in a loud drawl, "Ef y'all so damned smart, how come you goin' to 'Nam?" The next guy started on the game, and I sneaked away to get a beer. I returned to the funeral quiet barracks later, and was sitting at my bunk, reading an old copy of the *New Yorker* magazine, when an MP (military policeman) came over to my bunk and said, "PFC Keating, follow me."

I followed him outside the barracks to a small shack labeled "Military Police." The sky was turning from dark blue to black. There were ten or so other guys standing there. A big overweight MP sergeant came out and said, "All of you are non-commissioned officers [which was news to me, a PFC, private, first class!] and we need you to police the fence line. Guys are jumping the fence and going AWOL, trying to get out of going over to 'Nam, and you gotta help us out. We're short-handed on this holiday weekend. You will be issued a helmet liner, a nightstick, flashlight and whistle. Sergeant Smith will give your assigned area and times."

A voice from the group asked, "Sergeant, what if we catch someone, whadda we do?"

"Any crap happens, blow your whistle. Try to stop the guy," he said. "Use your nightstick if you have to, to protect yourself." Another MP Sergeant came out with a clipboard and started reading off names. He came to my name.

"Keating, you are on tomorrow at 1100 to 1200 hours, and then again at 2000 to 2100 hours." He finished reading the list and said, "Master Sergeant Hollis and me and my guys will be around, to check on you and to assist if you blow your whistles."

I stood in line to receive my white helmet liner, a black armband with the white letters "MP" on it, a nightstick, whistle and flashlight. I said to the sergeant as I was handed the gear, "I didn't know PFCs were noncoms." He nodded and said, "They were in the old Army."

I took my equipment back to my bunk and covered it with my blanket because I didn't want the other soldiers to know about my assignment. The next morning, just before 1100 hours, I headed over to the fence line near the MP shack, wearing my white helmet liner and armband, and carrying my nightstick and whistle. The clouds were darker now, and it looked like it was going to rain. I walked up and down the line but nothing happened. A real MP came by a couple of times, and we nodded to each other.

I was scheduled for another shift at 2000 hours. I was off to the fence line again, but this time it was different. Darkness all around, except for the glare of lights near the fence. A cold wind picked up. Groups of GIs were milling around, throwing quick glances at me and the other fence guards. I knew something was going to happen.

Suddenly about eight guys started climbing the fence. I blew my whistle and yelled "Halt!" And blew my whistle again. They didn't stop, and some guys turned toward me to shut me up.

I raised my nightstick in self-defense as I backed away from them, tooting the hell out of my whistle in a rapid-fire series of tweets. The real MPs showed up just in time, before they could rough me up.

The fence climbers got up and away. After things settled down, the MP sergeant came over and relieved me of further duty. "We'll get them tomorrow. They got nowhere to go," he said, as I turned back to the barracks, breathing hard but happy it was over.

My flight was posted for the next day, after Labor Day, so I went over to the telephone exchange to call home one more time and let them know.

When I got to the telephone, I dialed my home. My mother was upset, of course. My Dad repeated his warning not to volunteer for anything. I assured him I wouldn't. I said goodbye, and went back to the barracks and listened to my small Sony portable radio.

The next morning, after breakfast and one last administrative checkout, I boarded the bus to McGuire Air Force Base next to Fort Dix, the clouds darkening the sky. I was one of 170 other guys delivered to a waiting Boeing 707, emblazoned with the name "Flying Tiger Air" on it. Everyone was quiet. We dropped our duffels on the black tarmac like sandbags. We were given little paper tags with *"Bien Hoa Vietnam"* printed on them in red letters. We wrote our name and serial number on the tags, and tied them to our duffels. Everyone hand-carried their personnel files in a large manila envelope onto the plane.

The cabin filled fast. Officers were seated up front, and enlisted ranks filled the rest of the seats. Our cabin crew was staffed by four flight attendants, older than the usual pretty young attendants. I thought maybe they picked them because they looked like they were mothers and we wouldn't be unruly. I thought of Kathy in her bright yellow pantsuit. My trip to the war began.

CHAPTER 17

Welcome to Vietnam

The plane took off and headed west. This was a military flight, no movies, no music, no alcohol. We did have a meal, but I think it was sandwiches and cans of soda. I brought two books to read during the flight: John Barth's *The Sot-Weed Factor* and my copy of *Kiss Kiss Bang Bang*. I don't remember much about the flight, except feeling curious and nervous about what I would do when I got to the war. I kept my head in my book so I didn't have to think about what awaited me.

After a seven-hour flight to California for refueling, our plane continued on to Hawaii, another refueling stop. Many of us were asleep when the pilot announced that we were nearing Hawaii. His announcement woke us up and we all strained to look out the windows to see the Islands as the plane approached, large green lumps of land swimming in a blue sea, white clouds perched above them.

The plane had to be clear of passengers for the refueling, so they herded us into the terminal to wait. There was a flight returning from Vietnam, also refueling, and the bar was full of soldiers heading home. They saw us in our new jungle fatigues, and hooted at us "newbies."

I bought a postcard to send to Kathy, wrote a note on it, and dropped in the mailbox near the bar. One of the returning soldiers bought me a drink, asked me where I was going.

I told him Long Binh, and he assured me, "No sweat, that place is pretty safe."

Two hours later, after a quick meal of hamburgers and beer in the bar, we re-boarded and headed west, first to Guam for more fuel, and then the Republic of Vietnam. A total of twenty-seven hours in the air. When the plane arrived near the coast of Vietnam, our pilot announced that we would circle for a while because our destination, Bien Hoa Air Base, was under enemy fire. That woke us up and everyone looked out the windows, trying to see the battle, but our plane was above the clouds.

The plane began its final approach, in a steep dive and pulling up to land hard. It taxied quickly toward a terminal building. The door opened, and the flight attendants nervously hurried us off the plane in the dark. It was almost 2200 hours.

The heat and smells of Vietnam—a mix of motor oil, garbage, rice paddies, and shit from the water buffaloes assaulted me as I left the plane. The oppressive, wet heat soaked my new jungle fatigues with rivulets of sweat. I boarded a green school bus. Chain link fencing replaced the window glass to prevent hand grenades from being tossed inside. MPs in jeeps equipped with M60 machine guns, and wearing flak vests and steel helmets, drove alongside the buses. Off we went in the middle of the night to 90th Replacement Center, next to the Long Binh Post, a big base northeast of Saigon.

The intense tropical heat and humidity and the odors intensi-fied as the buses drove by rice paddies. We pulled into a barbed wire and sandbag enclosure at Long Binh Post. Dripping with sweat, we were told to assemble at a large dirt field, dropping our heavy duffel bags at our feet, soaking wet in our new jungle fatigues. This late at night the heat was unbearable. An officer with a bullhorn began to tell us about in-processing when sirens went off. He and his staff ran off. "Incoming!" someone yelled. We stood there, confused.

"Over here! Hey! New guys!" a sergeant shouted, and we ran to some sandbag bunkers. I squeezed into one of them. We heard the *crump! crump!* of exploding mortar or rocket shells. I counted three of them. Then they stopped. Someone said, "Welcome to Vietnam." A nervous laugh swept through the crowded bunker as guys released their fear. Another siren went off.

"All clear," someone said. "Everybody out!"

I could smell the acrid odor of cordite, adding another scent to my nose. I was in a war now. We assembled in the field, next to our deserted duffel bags. We were ushered into a large tin-roofed shed with benches but no walls. We placed our personnel files on the benches, and the clerk told us to write our names, blood type (in case our dog tags get blown up, he joked), home address, and the name of the school or college we attended, if we did. Write that down, too he said.

I thought to myself, Stonehill College in Massachusetts, the small, liberal arts Catholic school nobody ever heard about. I wrote it down anyway, what the hell. Then they divided us into groups of ten and led us over to a shed and made us apply an extremely strong, foul tasting fluoride paste to our teeth, a preventative against cavities. Apparently, the Army didn't want our teeth to get cavities during our tour. This thick metallic tasting tooth paste was supposed to fortify our teeth against cavities.

Just before dawn, the siren went off again when the Vietnamese fired some more rockets at us. I found out later that it was their pattern: rockets early morning, rockets early evening. The sun came up and we were able to eat a quick breakfast in the large mess hall. We ate real eggs, bacon, toast and coffee. Not bad for a war zone. I took a look around outside. The area was clear of any jungle, with lots of dusty red soil, and it was very flat. Tall barbed wire fences surrounded us, and a mix of large green tents, green wooden barracks and metal huts were scattered along thinly paved roads inside the perimeter.

Then we all formed up in the red clay field, at least one hundred of us, sweating as the heat rose with the sun. Huey helicopters were taking off nearby, dust clouds blooming under the *whop whop* of their rotors, which added to the noise of traffic around the base.

Across the open area near the buildings, I saw telephone poles, each with large round discs with unit emblems on them. A large red numeral "1" for the 1st Infantry Division, a Yellow Lightning Bolt on a red yellow leaf-shaped insignia for the 25th Infantry, and the yellow and black horse head of the 1st Cavalry among others units. When your name and unit were announced on the PA system, you were supposed to assemble at the pole with that unit emblem.

I spent three days here at the 90th Replacement Center. I was an unassigned soldier, with the I-A-O status as a conscientious objector. I was no longer an infantryman. Again, I wondered where I would be assigned. Maybe a fire base as a clerk, or hospital orderly or with graves registration somewhere. The sun rose higher in the sky, the temperature followed. For the next three days, after breakfast, we stood in the open field waiting for our names to be called. It was quite hot, and perspiration was pouring out of me. My jungle fatigues were soaked. After formation many of us were assigned work details around the base. I worked in the mess hall, setting up for meals, and cleaning pots and pans. Local Vietnamese workers in the mess hall made jokes about us "fucking new guys."

After three days of this routine, I heard my name over the loud speaker, "Keating, Thomas, PFC, report to the orderly room." I picked up my duffle and walked over to the Quonset hut, a small, barrel-shaped metal hut that was the orderly room. They were half-circular pre-fabricated structures, with curved metal roofs and walls, with wood front and back walls.

There were ten or so soldiers inside, at desks, phones chirping, piles of personnel folders in front of them, and typewriters and teletype machines. And it was air-conditioned! One of them, a slim specialist 4th class greeted me and offered his hand. He smiled and said, "So, you went to Stonehill College?" Surprised by the mention of my college, I just nodded and we shook hands.

"So did I. Graduated in '67, the year before you. Have a seat." I sat, wondering why I had been called out of formation.

"I do replacement assignments," he said, "and we can't have one of Stonehill's finest humping the boonies, now can we?" He smiled at me. "I got a need for a clerk typist over at 1st Log, that's Logistics, HQ [he pronounced it 'Haych Cue']. They're up the road. I can assign you there today. Whaddaya say?"

I didn't answer. I was confused and puzzled, and it showed on my face. He noticed and continued, "I caught your file; we look them over when you guys get the tooth treatment." He glanced down at it, "And when I saw Stonehill on the cover, I pulled it out for special assignment. I see you were in the seminary, we played you guys in touch football my senior year. You guys were tough." He smiled. "I see you're unassigned, formerly infantry, now I-A-O. You CAN type, right?"

"Yeah," I said, still reeling from what he said, adding, "I was a temporary company clerk at Fort Benning while I waited out my status decision."

He nodded and looking at the file said, "Okay, I see that a Sergeant Howell there gave you a good recommendation and changed your specialty to 71L, Administration." Sergeant Harrell had changed that for me back at Fort Benning.

"Good," he said. "Sit here while I type the new orders, and if everything works out, you'll spend your tour here in Long Binh."

"Wow," I said, "you can do this?"

"Hell, yeah, I've done this for other Stonehill guys since I've been here." He mentioned some names I knew, guys who graduated with me. My head was spinning as he picked up the phone. I heard him say, "...got you a very good typist. He's a college grad, history major, used to be a company clerk, knows his stuff. Okay, I'll send him up today." He put the phone down.

"That was the 47th's military history detachment's clerk, Jerry. You'll be working with him and the group. All set." I asked him how long he'd been in country.

"I'm short, got 30 days and a wake-up left in this place, and then I'm on the freedom bird to Boston." He smiled as he said that. "When you get settled, let me know how things work out up there at 1st Log."

He finished typing on the form, pressed a key, and the teletype machine clattered away. He looked at his watch.

"Your truck will be here in fifteen. You'll have to wait outside for it. Good luck." The printer stopped. He pulled a sheet off, and handed it to me. "Here's your new orders, good luck." We shook hands, and I thanked him again. I picked up my duffel and left the cool air and was blasted once again by the ungodly heat outside the hut. I waited for my ride. More helicopters were *whop whopping* the sky; more names were being called over at the parade ground. Ten minutes later, an olive-green drab Ford Econovan pulled up outside the hut. The driver said, "Keating?" and I nodded.

"Hop in, I'm Jerry." He drove out of the 90th Replacement and headed towards another base up on a hill. The 1st Logistical Command HQ was an air-conditioned, all metal, pre-fabricated building, the size of a two-story building, resting on a hill above some other buildings and tents. It was in the shape of a square, with a courtyard in the middle. There were green sandbagged bunkers located just outside the doors and around the building.

Jerry parked the van at the paved parking lot in the front. We went inside to cool air again, passed the armed MP on duty and went down a hallway to an office, where Jerry introduced me to the Commanding Officer, Colonel Woods, and 1st Sergeant Hollis, the senior noncommissioned officer, or NCO. After a few words with both, Jerry and I got back in the van and drove down the hill to the company area. He stopped in front of a group of long two-story wooden buildings, each with a tin roof, and open slat sides. A four-foot wall of sandbags and barrels filled with dirt surrounded the them, and there were sand bag bunkers at the front and rear door. A wooden sign that read "HHC Office" was in front of one of them. Jerry left me then and returned to the headquarters.

I signed in at the Headquarters Detachment barracks, or "hooch" as the soldiers called it. I was issued a helmet, web belt, canteen and straps ("web gear"), and a rifle serial number for a weapon I could not legally use since I was a noncombatant. The soldier at the armory hut told me to relax till I started work the next day. I started unpacking, and getting settled in my home for the next 365 days. I walked down past other hooches and found the Quonset hut, which was the day room or club for the company. This one was about one hundred feet long, with a window air-conditioner or two.

The bar was open and an older guy, a staff sergeant, was manning it. I asked for a beer, and got a bottle of beer, a brand I never heard of. It was cold. The Sergeant said the first one is free for newbies. The jukebox was playing "Lay, Lady, Lay" by Bob Dylan. I was surprised. That song was on the radios in July, Dylan sang it in August at the Isle of Wright concert, and here it was in Vietnam on September 5, 1969.

Sitting at a table, I sipped the beer and thought about where I was. Vietnam, war zone, combat zone. I was surprised at how hot it was here. The whole area was so busy. I wondered what was going to happen to me here. I was so thankful that Stonehill guy pulled my file and sent me here instead of a base camp or the morgue. It all happened so fast, it seemed. What happened to put me here? Last September I was working for Lou slinging hamburgers, trying to forget my seminary life, trying to start a career. Now I was in southeast Asia, in a war. I was scared. I remembered the rocket attack when I arrived three days ago. How many more of them would there be? Will I still be in this place in a month or so? Or out in some firebase counting drums of oil? I didn't know.

I finished the beer, thanked the Sergeant and went back outside in the heat and walked up the hill to my hooch. Vietnamese women who worked as laundry maids were all around, spreading wet laundry on the sandbag walls around the buildings. A large truck called a deuce and a half came down the road, stopped in front of a small lean-to, and about ten GIs hopped down, wearing helmets and flak jackets, and carrying M16s.

I didn't know what was happening, but one of them spotted me in my bright green new fatigues and said, "Coming off guard duty, newbie." I nodded, and watched as they unloaded their weapons, put the loaded magazines in an ammo box. The box went back on the truck, which drove away. The soldiers then dispersed to their different barracks. I knew I would not be carrying a weapon, but wondered what I would do on guard duty—be a litter bearer or maybe man the communications center? I was sure I would find out soon enough. I was in the war for the next year.

CHAPTER 18

Disneyland East

My war was fought in Long Binh Army Base, the largest military base outside the US. Thirty thousand soldiers lived on a large cleared area near a river, about fifteen miles northeast of Saigon. The ground had a reddish, clay color, the residue of defoliant application, Agent Orange, which cleared the jungle and under-growth. Long Binh was the center for all Logistical support for the war effort. The Post was nestled beside the Bien Hoa Air Base, the 101st Airborne Division headquarters, the US Army Vietnam headquarters, and the 1st Logistical Command headquarters.

The grunts, the combat soldiers, called us Rear Echelon Mother Fuckers, or REMFs. In contrast to their lives in the jungle, REMFs like me lived in relative comfort, with hot food, plenty of water and real beds. The closest I would come to combat duty was pulling bunker guard duty once every couple of weeks, out on the fence line facing the countryside, usually as duty driver.

The Post was a nice target for the enemy because it was so large. Any rocket or mortar fired into it was bound to hit something. I lived and worked in what the military called a hostile fire zone, and the Army paid me extra because our Post was under fire daily. Enemy rockets and mortars shelled us and they were constantly trying to attack us with commando raids. One got used to the alert sirens, waiting for the mortar or 122-millimeter rocket attacks to end, hearing the all clear sirens then returning to work. I was one of the support troops in this war.

Vietnam weather at Long Binh was hot and muggy. During the dry season, the heat of the day reached upwards of 100 degrees, and the humidity was around eighty percent. It was a little cooler during the monsoon season, but that was because it rained hard just about every day all day. I worked in a building that was air-conditioned, but everywhere else I went, it was hot and humid. Cold at work, terrifically hot and humid elsewhere.

We were usually awakened by sirens indicating incoming fire around dawn as the Viet Cong would fire two or three 122 mm Russian or Chinese-made rockets at targets on the base. One of those rockets hit my hooch. I was lucky that day because I was eating early breakfast over at the mess hall up at the top of the small hill in the company area. No one was injured, but there was large hole where a sandbag shelter, or bunker, stood before being hit.

My duty shift began around 0700 hours, after a breakfast and short drive to the headquarters building up on the hill. The headquarters for all logistics and supply in the country was a pre-fabricated metal two-story building, air-conditioned with a tarmac parking lot in front.

My job at the 47th Military History Detachment was to type transcripts of recorded interviews with different logistical teams around the country. The interviews were conducted by the officers in the detachment, and us clerks would type the transcripts or reports of those interviews. The Army was compiling a history of logistical supplies in the war, and our officers would travel all over Vietnam with their tape recorders and interview supply officers.

We were commanded by Colonel Woods, formerly of the Hawaiian National Guard and a World War II and Korean War veteran. He was about fifty-five years old. His command consisted of five officers, four majors and one captain, and four enlisted men. The enlisted men consisted of a Platoon Sergeant, and three enlisted men, myself, Jerry and Rich. Later our enlisted staff would be increased by the addition of Loren and James.

Two civilian employees of the Department of Defense were also assigned to our group. They provided the contractor's view of the supply effort. These civilians were expert in black market deals, enriching themselves by purchasing goods in the PX and selling them on the black market during their time in country. Later in my tour I had other duties, with other units, but basically the headquarters was my workplace.

Work ended around six or seven PM. If we had no extra duty, the night was ours. We ate all our meals in the company mess hall. Our meals were pretty good as far as Army standards went, and we did have fresh eggs and bread, and steaks once in a while. Most of the vegetables were canned or frozen, the potatoes were the instant mix type. Nobody complained because we knew the infantry units were eating canned rations in jungle settings. There was a small diner-type café up at the headquarters complex, and if we could, we would grab lunch there. The café was run by Vietnamese staff who would shout at you if you didn't order fast enough. 'Hamma-Chee' was a popular item, a ham and cheese sandwich.

After dinner there were things to do to keep us occupied. There was a small outdoor theater in the next company area built out of sandbags and lumber. Movies were shown there most nights.

The films were mostly B movies, and some A-listed ones. Films like *The Italian Job*, *Sweet Charity*, and *Butch Cassidy and the Sundance Kid*, but usually we had bad Burt Reynolds and Charles Bronson westerns. One film that was very popular and played often was a French film called *The Last Adventure*, starring Alain Delon and Joanna Shimkus. She was the reason the movie was so popular with us. She played a carefree adventurer sailing around off the coast of Africa in her bikini. Many times, our films were interrupted by sirens and incoming rockets, and we had to run to bunkers till the all clear sounded.

A small outdoor theater nearby usually had a band most nights, mostly Filipino rock bands attempting to sing songs from the Beatles, Rolling Stones, Beach Boys, and so on. They sang in butchered English. Each performance ended with a rousing rendition of "We Gotta Get Outta This Place" by the Animals, a favorite tune for guys in the war zone.

The last choice for the night would be over at the Engineer Company area, where the engineers built a nice combination bar and bomb shelter. Beer was cheaper there than the enlisted men's (EM) club, and it was a relaxed, non-military atmosphere. It was small, so you had to arrive early to find a bench to sit down. I spent many nights there, shooting the breeze with Jimmy or Loren.

Back in the hooch at night, guys played cards or read books, Armed Forces Radio, Vietnam (AFVN) blaring rock on Japanese portable radios, or just sat around bullshitting about their lives before the Army. Sometimes the company would receive remaindered paperback books or model kits of planes, cars, and things like that. We would try to put them together; in spite of the fact the directions were in Japanese.

Sleep was always a challenge. We slept on bunks with thin mattresses, in tropical air and humidity. There was the continual reports of artillery and flares, and machines guns out on the perimeter each night, which constantly woke me from sleep. Of course, it was still nothing like sleeping on the jungle floor, like the infantry.

The heat and humidity each night was a problem. We slept on top of the mattress and sheet; it was too hot to cover up. Those who could bought table fans to move the wet air around their bunk, or they could "rent" one from Dutch. Dutch was an enlisted guy who was a scrounger and wheeler-dealer. He trafficked in black market goods like cigarettes, alcohol, and small appliances. Fans and small refrigerators were his specialty. I suppose every Army unit in the support troop areas had a guy like him. Where he got his goods was a mystery to me. He sold cold beer and soft drinks from one of his refrigerators. I occasionally bought some beer from him. Dutch was a big guy who played football in a midwestern big-time college, and even tried out for the Green Bay Packers. Unfortunately for Dutch, Army MPs caught him with too many ration cards (soldiers were supposed to have only one), and he got shipped off to jail, a week before he was due to leave Vietnam.

One of my primary duties was duty driver for the headquarters company. I had to pass an international driver's license test, know the road signs and right of ways. Luckily, we drove on the right side of the road, so the driving test was easily passed. I had a Jeep assigned to me, and it was my job to drive the officers and pick up supplies, and sometimes be a messenger to and from other unit headquarters on the large base. It was important to me that the jeep was in top running order, in case I needed to get out of the way of trouble. I always performed oil changes, and tire changes to be in top form. Rarely did I drive outside the wire of the huge base.

Our barracks were hot and humid at night, and very hot and humid during the day. Usually we wore only our green t-shirts and boxer shorts in the barracks. Some guys bought fans and small refrigerators from the mail order PX in Japan, and that helped. We had showers and bathrooms in an open communal bath area. The Vietnamese mama-sans would just walk through the area doing the laundry and point at our nakedness and make jokes about us, giggling.

Speaking of money, the legal tender for GIs was Military Payment Certificates, or MPC. MPC was equal to US dollars, ten MPC dollars was worth ten dollars in American money. The "greenback" currency in the US is an international currency. However, to prevent the Viet Cong from acquiring US dollars and using them to purchase weapons or finance other nefarious tasks, US personnel all got paid in MPCs each month.

Every once in a while, the Army changed the MPC currency, or converted it, which meant we had to turn in our old MPCs for new ones. Vietnamese currency was the Dong/Piaster, which could be bought with the MPCs, but nobody really wanted the currency of the country, even the Vietnamese. The Military Payment Certificate was the only money that could buy anything. Of course, the black market loved MPCs, and American whiskey and cigarettes, especially menthol flavored smokes like Newports. We used Newports as cash to pay for any number of jobs the local nationals performed. They made a good profit by selling them on the black market.

There was a constant reminder of how much better life was at Long Binh than in firebases and in the combat units. We had two major field hospitals on our base which were receiving wounded continuously. My hooch was located near the 24th EVAC (Evacuation) hospital, a 1969 version of a MASH unit. It was a cluster of tents and pre-fabricated buildings. Helicopters carrying wounded, called Dust Offs, would fly in 24-7, at treetop level, with wounded. Sometimes we could look over there and see the Army nurses taking a break smoking outside the EVAC, their hospital garb smeared with somebody's blood.

CHAPTER 19

Goddam Taxes

My only real combat experience, aside from incoming rockets, came in February of 1970 while I was on guard duty. I was the guard duty driver. My job that night was to drive the officer of the guard ("OG") to the bunker line to check on the guys guarding the perimeter of the base.

I drove the duty jeep to the officers' quarters to pick up Major Smith, a logistics officer who was assigned that day as officer of the guard. Our job for the next twenty-four hours was to check on the soldiers pulling guard duty in the bunkers along our sector of the base perimeter, especially at night, guarding against attack by the Viet Cong, our enemy.

Wearing our steel helmets and flak vests, the Major checked out his sidearm, while I checked our PRC-25 radio and our call sign ("Rover 6") at the guard shack before starting the first of three or four runs. My flak vest reeked of the sweaty odor of the guy who wore it before me. The major had his own personal flak vest. I threw mine into the back seat of the jeep along with my helmet. Too warm and muggy to wear the heavy vest and helmet. I wore my soft cap wide-brimmed "boony hat" instead.

Our perimeter sector covered ten bunkers along a stretch of the perimeter. Each bunker had room for four to six soldiers, who were support troop: truck drivers, typists, payroll clerks, most with little or no combat training or experience.

I was not impressed with the skills these guys displayed. Even though I was now a noncombatant, I did excel in Infantry School. These men were not comfortable with the weapons in their hands. I saw how clumsy they were when they would carry their weapons. In the infantry I was taught to be comfortable with the M16, always have it ready to use. The rifles were not very clean, either. M16s had to be cleaned regularly to work properly. These guys probably fired their weapons once or twice. I fired my weapon every day for eight weeks in the infantry and was accustomed to it.

They had their weapons, a field telephone, gas lamp and large water bag, and M-60 machines guns in every other bunker. Piss tubes made from rocket packing tubes were driven into the soil outside and behind the bunker for urination. A shovel was provided for defecation disposal. Guys usually brought their own toilet paper.

A dirt road behind the perimeter line allowed jeeps and trucks and any armored vehicle access, but tonight it was just our duty jeep. The darkness and the humid air shrouded us as we drove out toward the line of bunkers. The stars above were brilliant white. My jeep had small "cat's-eye" lights, which were headlights covered by a screen that allowed only a dim light so you could see the road.

When we pulled up to the first bunker, the Officer of the Guard announced his presence by saying the first part of the password, i.e., "Bearcat" and the reply from the guard inside would be "mountain" or something like that. I normally would stay in the jeep, engine always running, in case we had to move fast. After his inspection, the OG would come back out, hop in the jeep and off we'd go to the next bunker. We did this twice during the night, and twice during the day. Each trip took about ninety minutes. We had just left bunker 6 when the Major had me stop the jeep so he could take a piss. I got out and stretched my legs.

We were between bunkers, but still behind the berm. Lights from trucks behind us back in the center of the busy Post briefly cast light on us. The Major finished his business and turned to the jeep when we heard *WHISST* as something flew past my head, then almost at the same time, a gunshot. We dove behind the jeep.

"Jeezus!" said the Major. He reached up into the jeep and got the handset of the PRC radio.

The major pressed the talk key and called, "Bearcat 1, Rover 6."

"Rover 6," the command bunker acknowledged.

The major replied, "Bearcat 1, incoming rifle fire, single round near Bearcat 6 and 7, coming from the village, negative whiskeys." (In Army lingo, no wounded.)

"Rover 6, roger incoming. Negative whiskeys, continue patrol," the command bunker replied.

"Bearcat 1," acknowledged the Major, and put the handset back.

"Meet me at bunker 7," he said to me and ran, bent low, over to the bunker.

I slid back into the jeep and turned towards the back seat and put on my sweat-stained and smelly flak vest, and my helmet. Bending low, I put the Jeep in first gear and drove to bunker 7. This time, I went in with him as he inspected the guard. Two guys were snoozing, and the other two stood as we entered.

"Anything to report?" the Major asked.

"We heard a shot about five minutes ago and called it into Bearcat 1, and they said it came from the village," replied one of the soldiers.

"Roger that," said the Major. "Someone took a shot at us."

Both soldiers looked at each other. They were puzzled. The village facing the perimeter was quiet and they hadn't seen any activity out there. The major started his inspection. The soldiers on guard duty had loaded weapons, the phone was function-ing, they knew their call signs, and they had their water and C-rations, so we left. We finished the first circuit of inspections and arrived at the command bunker, Bearcat 1.

The Bearcat 1 bunker was taller and twice as big as the regular ones we inspected, a couple of antennas atop the roof, and there were M-60 machine guns in two of the gun ports, and two or three radio sets, command nets monitored by a soldier wearing a headset. Bearcat was manned by experienced combat infantrymen from the 199th Light Infantry Brigade. They were on the last month of their combat tour and were reward-ed with this light duty. They had a starlight scope, early night vision technology on a tripod and positioned in another gun port. After saluting the Major, the young lieutenant in charge said,

"Sir, want to see who took a shot at you?"

"You know who it is?"

"Oh yeah, it was definitely Uncle Ho, that's what we call him," replied the Lieutenant.

The major said, "Who the fuck is that?"

The Lieutenant replied, "He's the village elder, the chief. He comes out every couple of hours at night and takes a shot or two at our bunker line. He doesn't hit anything, though." Looking at his watch, he said, "It's almost 2000 hours and he should be back. Take a look through the starlight."

The major peeked through the scope, "I don't see anything." He moved the scope. "Wait a second. There's an old guy on the roof of that house with a weapon."

"That's Uncle Ho. He's got a Japanese army rifle from World War II. I don't know how he gets ammo for it, but that's what he shoots."

The major straightened up, and said, "Keating, take a look."

I bent down to the scope and saw in the green and gray screen an old man ("papa-san") wearing trousers and a long-sleeved shirt. He lifted a funny looking rifle up to his shoulder, pointed it towards our perimeter, then fired off a round. We heard the shot as it rang out. I kept my eye on the scope as the old man put the rifle down and began climbing down off his roof. I stood up. The major turned to the lieutenant and said, "Why are you letting him do that?"

The Lieutenant smiled and said, "It's because of, you know, that 'win their hearts and minds shit.' The old man is paying his taxes to the Viet Cong. As long as he shoots at us each night, they won't take all the rice from his village, or kidnap the young men for combat. We ain't allowed to fire back, at least not until he hits someone,"—he caught himself, "Sir."

The Major shook his head. "Well, he came close tonight, didn't he Keating?"

"Damn close, sir." I said.

We gave the Lieutenant the inspection report for this run and went to the jeep to head back to the base guard shack to rest before the next inspection round. I started the jeep and I heard the Major mutter "Goddamn Taxes" as we drove away.

CHAPTER 20

Mimi and John

The war was quiet in the Saigon Military District in June of 1970. Most of the action was in Cambodia and the border. We were busy at my base in Long Binh trying to get the supplies the combat troops needed in Cambodia. I was told to go to Saigon to deliver some documents to the MACV (Military Assistance Command, Vietnam) headquarters, the supreme military HQ in country, and it was located in the heart of Saigon.

I was in Saigon once before, and looked forward to visiting the city again. I drove there with Joe, who had been to the city many times and knew it well. Saigon even in wartime was very busy. Vietnamese police, dressed in white uniforms (GIs called them White Mice) kept the heavy civilian and military traffic flowing through the city. We arrived at the MACV headquarters building near the American Embassy, and I escorted Joe as he dropped the document bag off to the MACV offices. That done, we had the afternoon to take some time for fun in the city.

Joe headed over to the infamous Tu Do street, near the Cholon district. Tu Do street was the place where prostitutes, black market shops and bath houses were located among the restaurants and shops. Black market goods were readily available, for the right price. You could buy anything in the shops: French perfume, German cameras, US Army uniforms, even weapons.

An array of little shops and old French Beaux Arts buildings dotted both sides of the wide avenue. There were some black ugly gaps in the rows of shops, reminders of the house-to-house fighting last year in the city. The street was busy with people walking. "Off Limits" signs were posted everywhere by the Military Police. I saw a lot of GIs walking and shopping, ignoring the signs.

Being in Saigon again was another opportunity for me. I fancied myself a writer and I wanted to experience the sins of Saigon, adding to my cachet as a writer in wartime. All my religious ties to the seminary and religion had disappeared after almost two years in the Army. Earlier in the year, I gave up my seminarian virginity in one of the bath houses during my first trip to Saigon. The steam bath was great, and the prostitute was very efficient. She led me to the table, pulled off her clothes and my towel.

"Me love you long time, GI," she said, and hopped on the table. I joined her and did what the Vietnamese call *sự giao cấu* (we fucked). It was my first time. The intense pleasure lasted a few seconds, and then it was over. I was awed by the sexual act I had just completed. Years of celibate life disappeared in that bath house. I gave her the cash, cleaned myself and got dressed. The steam bath houses and prostitutes shared the same old French Beaux Arts buildings. You could have a nice steam bath and a good time girl (prostitute) for a single price, maybe ten dollars MPC (military payment currency).

This time I didn't want a bath. I wanted to get a different real-life experience and write about it. Tu Do street was my destination. Joe dropped me off and pointed down a little side street.

"You get better prices for the girls, here," he said. "Take your pick, I gotta go see a friend," he winked. "I'll be back in an hour to pick you up here."

I walked down the street and saw a small storefront with a blue door, part of a partitioned old colonial era building. I entered without knocking. Inside was a really little bedroom that held a bed, a sink, and an old upholstered chair. The room was clean and neat. US Army issue stuff was sprinkled all around—a couple of small green t-shirts and an Army wide-brimmed bush hat hung on back of the door. Two green, unopened C-ration cans of peaches and a folded Army poncho liner were on a small table near the bed. A small Sony radio on the table was playing rock and roll music, tuned to the Armed Forces Radio Vietnam (AFVN) station.

The room was lit by a bare light bulb hung from the high ceiling. I saw some photos of helicopters and Air Force fighter planes taped on the wall over the bed. The back wall displayed a faded black and white picture of President Kennedy. Curtains hid another small room, probably a toilet or a small kitchen. There was an electric fan on the table moving back and forth.

A young woman greeted me and said her name was Mimi. She looked to be seventeen-years old, and was five feet tall and slim, not skinny. Her face was clear and smooth, with jet black hair that fell to her shoulders. She was wearing a one-piece shift with a flowery pattern and buttons down the front. She smiled and said, "You want Mimi? I am five dollahs one time, OK?"

I nodded yes and reached into my pocket for five military pay script dollars. After I handed her the money, she started to unbutton my fatigue shirt, a signal for me to undress. When I finished undressing, Mimi smiled and unbuttoned her shift, and put it on the chair. Her small naked body and yellow skin was as flawless as her face. She smiled when she saw me naked and ready. I was calm. I considered myself an expert in sex even though this was the second time for me. I noticed that her breasts had tattooed names on them, done with crude blue lettering. Mimi on one, John on the other.

We climbed onto the bed as the radio started to play "Bridge over Troubled Water." She lay back and I entered her body. She was smiling as I shuddered with pleasure, and I finished before the song ended. I lifted off her and the bed, went over to the chair, sat down and reached for my clothes. I was happy. I was now sexually experienced. Mimi came off the bed toward me. She brought me a damp cloth and I started to clean myself. I pointed to her breasts and asked her, "Who is John?"

She smiled and said, "John is American Air Force, he stay with me whole year. He is coming back for me and take me to US," she said, smiling. Then she proudly stated, "He has same tattoo."

Air Force meant he was assigned right here in Saigon at Tan San Nhut Airport. I was angry at the lying bastard. He used her for sex for a year, telling her he would come back for her. He was never coming back. My god, she believed John was coming back! This guy John is home in the US with his wife, probably. Jesus!

All I could say was, "Good for you two, I hope you have a happy life." My comment pleased her, and she came over and perched on my lap and reached down and slipped me into her again.

"You nice GI, this time no charge," she said. She began to rock slowly, her tattooed breasts inches from my face. Mimi and John bounced three inches from me. I tried to enjoy her once again, but I just couldn't get that bastard John out of my head. He probably shared her with other airmen, like he was a pimp. He was a bastard, alright. Without warning, I lost my stiffness. So much for being sexually experienced. Damn it! I gently moved her off me. She was puzzled. I rushed to put on my fatigues.

"Mimi, I gotta go back to MACV," I lied, and reached into my pocket for some money. I had about $30 in MPC. I gave her all of it.

She took the money, still confused, but said, "OK, you go GI," and slipped on her shift. She opened the door for me and I left.

I hurried up the alley to the corner. The hour was almost up and Joe wasn't there at the corner. No jeep, and I noticed that there were no GIs anywhere. The MPs must be nearby. I was getting nervous. Not good being the only US soldier on THIS street. An MP could arrest me, or worse, one of the White Mice. I looked at my watch. 1600 hours. We were due back at Long Binh at 1800 hours. I started walking up Tu Do street past the shops trying to remember where the MACV office was located. Up ahead of me I saw a young ARVN (Vietnamese soldier) getting on a Vespa motor scooter. He looked young, maybe sixteen. He was wearing Vietnamese Army fatigues, had corporal stripes on his sleeve and wore a wide-brimmed hat. Using my very poor Vietnamese I shouted "*Lái xe cho tôi trụ sở chính! lái xe cho tôi trụ sở chính!!*" (Drive me to headquarters!), hoping he knew where MACV was.

He nodded and I hopped on the back of his Vespa. The young soldier weaved in and out of the heavy Saigon traffic with ease, scuttling along the edge of the street, turning quickly to avoid pedestrians, and then zooming between the trucks and buses while I hung onto him absolutely scared that he was going to get us killed. My arms were wrapped tight around his waist. The corporal paid no attention to road courtesy, finding gaps in the stream of traffic, speeding up and slowing when an obstacle like a bus got in his way. He was on a mission.

Ten scary minutes later, we pulled up in front of the MACV building. I got off the scooter and when I put my hand in my pocket to give him some money, I remembered I had given it all to Mimi. The only thing I had left was a half pack of Marlboros and my Zippo lighter. I gave them to him and said "*Cảm on bạn*" (Thank you). I started walking toward the building when I heard a jeep horn. I turned to see Joe stop behind me in the jeep. He apologized for being late, said his "friend" kept him busier and longer than he planned. He gave me another wink. He asked me if I had a good time with the good time girl.

"It was okay," I said. "Real nice girl."

I didn't tell him about her tattoos. That night I wrote down the events of the day in my journal, and about Mimi and John. I wrote "John used her all year for sex, and then went home. He was a sonofabitch for doing that to Mimi." I looked at what I wrote and added; "Hell, I used her too, so I guess I'm a sonofabitch. This fuckin' war can make you be a sonofabitch." I closed my journal. I made a couple more trips to MACV HQ in Saigon during my time in Vietnam. I never went back to the shop with the blue door.

CHAPTER 21

A Convoy for the Con Voi

In March of 1970, I was re-assigned to a different headquarters unit at Long Binh Post. I wasn't on the job long when my commanding officer called me in and said, "Keating, go with Joe and get my elephants."

"Sir?" I asked puzzled. He looked at me for a second, then he remembered I was the new guy. He explained. The Colonel was leaving Vietnam soon and had ordered some decorative, ceramic elephants from a local factory to bring home to Georgia.

These elephants were made of china or clay, fired and glazed and brightly colored. They were hollow like a chocolate Easter bunny. They stood about one meter high and people used them as plant stands in their homes.

GIs called them Big Ugly Fucking Elephants, and my Colonel wanted me to drive to the factory somewhere in the countryside, pick up the elephants and bring them back to his quarters before he went home.

The local factory was about 20 kilometers (klicks) from our base. It was in the middle of nowhere, and near a US Army combat base. That was not good. I knew that combat bases were always located where the enemy was most active in an area.

Joe, an E-5 sergeant who had been there on other trips, was gonna be the driver. The idea was to show me the way to the factory so I could do the next trip for the officers. While he signed out the jeep and his weapon, I put four canteens of water in the back of the jeep. We joined a small MP truck convoy that was going to the combat base near the factory. The convoy commander, a young lieutenant, called all the drivers together to go over the basic rules of the convoy.

"Keep your interval between vehicles. Don't let any fucking gook vehicles in the convoy, or ARVNs, either. Never stop, no matter what. If fired on, speed up and get the fuck out of the kill zone. Got it?"

Everyone nodded. Convoys were always a target. The truck drivers and their relief drivers carried M-16 automatic rifles. They sat on their armor-plated flak vests as extra protection against what are nowadays call IEDs, but back then we called them command detonated mines. Joe and I sat on our vests.

Our convoy went out the main gate of the base, the Lieutenant in the lead in his jeep with its M-60 machine gun on the mount. Another jeep brought up the rear, also with a machine gunner.

I thought, nobody back home would believe that I was in an armed convoy going to an enemy-held area to get fucking ceramic elephants for an officer's mid-century ranch-style house in Georgia. Great.

As we turned onto Highway 1, Joe pointed out an elderly, bearded Vietnamese man wearing a *Non La*, the famous Asian conical hat made of reeds, sitting by the side of the road.

"See that papa-san?" he said. "He's counting the vehicles in this convoy. He'll report to the Viet Cong how many vehicles we have, and where we're heading, north or south. There's a gook at every exit on the Post." I looked over at the old man—he was using his Buddhist beads to count our trucks.

The convoy moved slowly. The tropical sun beat on us, but the slight breeze as we drove gave us some relief. We had travelled about one kilometer into the trip, when I heard a sharp screeching sound up ahead, then a blaring truck horn, followed by a loud crunch. The convoy speeded up. We did the same. As we zipped ahead, I saw a crushed Vespa motor scooter in the middle of the road. One of the trucks in the convoy had run over it. It must have slipped between the trucks.

I didn't see the Vespa driver, but there was a lot of blood on the road, and a smear of blood led off to the shoulder where a cluster of Vietnamese was shouting at the convoy.

"*Dung Lai! Dung Lai!*" ("Stop! Stop!") Nobody stopped. We drove on.

An hour later, Joe turned off the highway and onto a rut-filled dirt road, red dust spilling behind us. We were in the "boonies," some place in the middle of rice paddies and jungle.

The elephant "factory" was a low rambling one-story structure made from sheets of corrugated metal. Two ceramic elephants were standing on either side of the entrance. A hand-painted sign in Vietnamese said CON VOI ("Elephants") over the entrance. Joe parked the jeep and entered the factory to check on our elephants while I stood guard at the jeep in the hot sun.

I took off my helmet and put on my wide brimmed boonie hat, and was drinking from a canteen when some Vietnamese kids from the little village next to the factory gathered around the jeep. They were all thin, black haired and smiling. They asked for cigarettes with the universal sign language of two fingers at the mouth. I obliged and passed out my Marlboros.

One kid, about seven years old, begged for a cigarette and I gave him one. I laughed when he whipped out a Zippo lighter to light his buddies' cigarettes.

I showed them a magic trick I learned from watching old Laurel and Hardy movies, where Stan would seem to take off his finger and put it back on. They shrieked and laughed at the trick and wanted me to do it again. They spoke no English, but, using my bad Vietnamese, I did get them to count, *một, hai, ba*, before I put my finger back together a few more times.

Joe returned with the workers and they carefully placed our two brightly colored elephants into the jeep. After covering them with a canvas tarp, I gave the kids the rest of my Marlboros and we drove away.

It was getting late, and we didn't want to drive back to Long Binh Post alone, at night. Nighttime belonged to the VC. We checked in at the combat base near the factory for the night. The MP at the gate told us to keep any weapons handy. Intel indicated possible enemy activity.

We didn't get much sleep that night, awakened by artillery fire and the sound of flares popping into the darkness, and the *brrappp*! of miniguns firing red lines of bullets down from gunships onto some poor bastards outside the perimeter. I guess Army Intel was right for once. Our elephants were snug and covered in the back of the jeep.

When we left the base the next morning, sure enough, I saw an old man sitting outside the gate, watching and counting. We returned to Long Binh and Joe drove to the officers' quarters where we dropped the elephants off at the Colonel's air-conditioned trailer.

A few days later, he shipped his two ceramic elephant stands home and left Vietnam three days later.   Before he left, the Colonel wrote recommendations for medals for both of us for getting the elephants.

His recommendations were "For Hazardous Duty" on the citation.   Thankfully,   higher   headquarters   denied   the recommendations. It would be so embarrassing to have to tell people, "And I got this medal here for delivering plant stands."

I never had to drive back to the factory, the village, and the kids. The factory owner started selling his elephants in a shop on our base not long after that first trip. He was doing great business when I went home three months later—without any elephants.

CHAPTER 22

Popcorn and Death

I suppose the strangest duty I had was night watch, when the cleaning teams of Vietnamese women—we called them "mama-sans"—came to clean the office building. One of America's nation-building efforts during my time there was to hire local national workers to perform jobs so that GIs could be free to do their jobs. Every couple of weeks I had to stand watch while they mopped floors, cleaned windows, emptied trash, and so on, to be sure none of them was going to plant a booby trap under a desk.

They all pretended not to speak any English, which was just their way of not having to deal with us. I discovered this one night when I cooked some popcorn that my girlfriend had sent in a care package to me. It was one of those Jiffy Pop stove-top products that you put on a hot plate and let the popcorn pop and fill the aluminum foil balloon. They had never seen that before, and two of them asked me, "What THAT?" And, "What popcorn? Me no know."

So, I knew they had some English. I shared the popcorn with them, and they loved it. I was now a "numbah one GI."

Long Binh, being a big and central operations location, was always having rockets launched against it, usually in the morning or just after, but the larger threat came from sappers. Viet Cong sappers were commandos, highly trained

110

soldiers whose missions were to sneak into our base, through the barbed wire, the mine fields and even the bunker line, to plant explosives, or kill soldiers with their AK-47 rifles before getting killed or captured themselves.

While on guard duty one had to be alert for a sapper attack. Many times, we watched firefights outside our base, the enemy fire identified by green tracer rounds, ours by red tracer rounds. One night, a group of sappers tried to infiltrate our section of the base perimeter. A sharp-eyed soldier saw movement and fired a flare, which exposed them.

Automatic rifle and machine gun fire from other bunkers killed the four sappers. In the morning, when the detail went out to clean up the bodies, it was discovered that one of them, presumably the leader, was in fact one of the most popular barbers on the Post. Everyone had been to his barber shop, including officers. It was strange to think someone you talked to regularly, shared a joke or two, was trying to kill you. Security and night watch duty was increased after that incident. The evening watch continued, everyone more alert. I still made popcorn for the maids when I got packages from home, but things were different now. I was tense, and they were wary. I wasn't a "numbah one GI" anymore, just a GI.

After the war, it was clear that many of those "workers" were in fact enemy agents, providing all sorts of information to the North Vietnamese Army.

CHAPTER 23

R&R in the Land Down Under

April 1970 was an important month in my year in Vietnam. Nixon was in his first years as president, the Bruins had won the Stanley Cup, the Apollo 13 disaster was unfolding, and cigarette advertising got banned on American TV. All of that was insignificant because that month I was going on R&R!

R&R, or rest and recuperative leave, was offered to all soldiers in the Vietnam theater of operations. You were allowed six days leave out of the war zone each tour. While all soldiers were supposed to be able to take R&R, many combat troops were not able to do so. I had applied for R&R leave while working at headquarters in my new job as an aide to a Colonel. I had worked a variety of assignments in the headquarters before my assignment as an aide to Colonel Stone. He was sent to Vietnam for ninety days to boost his retirement pension. He had no assigned duty. He sat in his office calling all his buddies around different Vietnam bases by telephone, while I sat in the outer office reading books, lots of them. I drove him to and from his air-conditioned quarters each day, in an air-conditioned olive-green American Motors Javelin, and to the fancy restaurant or officer's club on base where officers and contractors congregated.

He approved my request for R&R for Sydney, Australia. I knew I probably would never get to Australia otherwise, and I wanted to go there. Deciding where to go was a challenge. Many guys went to Thailand, the sex capital of Asia. Others went to Japan, or Hong Kong, or Taiwan. Some even flew back to Hawaii to meet up with a wife or fiancé. I chose Sydney because Australia was the closest place that looked like the United States, and the people there spoke English. However, I soon discovered Australians spoke Australian, not English.

My friend, Bruce, another headquarters guy, also got approval from his commanding officer. Bruce was from Michigan, and had been in the auto industry as a management trainee when he got drafted. He was billeted in my barracks, and we had become friends due to our shared love of author John D. MacDonald books. Bruce wanted to go to Australia, too.

Bruce and I flew out of Bien Hoa Air Base on a Boeing 707, in April of 1970; the plane was full of GIs on R&R and Australian troops going home on leave. I sat next to an Aussie who must have been forty years old, and wore a private's stripes on his fatigues. He told me he had been busted for beating up a Vietnamese soldier in a bar in Vung Tao, where the Australian Army headquarters was located.

The long flight arrived in Sydney in their autumn, a bit cool. Bruce and I were processed in by US Army staff (that was their war duty, pretty good, I'd say), given IDs, and sent to a large room where donated civilian clothes were hanging on racks. The clothes weren't fashionable, but they were civilian clothes. I changed into the ones that fit, and I was able to take enough outfits for the week.

Now, it was great to be in a busy city, with people who dressed like we did, and we didn't have to be afraid of a grenade thrown at us. Bruce and I were assigned to a lovely little motel in an area of Sydney called Woolloomooloo, near Kings Cross, so we were in where the action was, clubs and bars and lots of fun.

We had plenty of cash, and the first place we went to was the Pink Pussycat bar, I believe it was called. Go-Go girls were dancing on the bar, in tasteful bikinis—this was 1970, remember. It was crowded and the bar jammed with other US soldiers in ill-fitting civilian clothes, drinking and gawking at the dancers. Loud Beatles music was blaring.

We bought our first Australian beer, which we found delightful, but it contained more alcohol than the American beer we were used to drinking. The music and the noise got to us, so we left and went to the USO center for information, picking up free tickets to shows, and date matching. Date matching went like this: A large group of young ladies would come to the USO center and meet with guys on R&R. If they liked each other, they left the center together for the week.

Bruce and I met with some young attractive young women who were pleasant and friendly. We were paired up for the week. Now, many guys shacked up with their dates in what today we would call hook-ups, but Bruce and I were proper young men. My young lady was named Margaret. She had red hair, wore mini-skirts, and had a pretty smile. The ladies were very good companions, great unofficial tour guides to the city. In return, all they wanted was to be wined and dined, and could we pay for their dry cleaning?

Through the USO, we could get tickets for nightclubs and the theater. The best tickets were for a show at some nightclub high atop some building downtown. The great Tony Bennett and Louie Belson were headlining. We got the tickets and met the girls at their apartment and took a cab to the club. The four of us rode in an elevator to the top floor where the club was located. We got in the elevator, and it stopped on the second floor for Mr. Bennett and Mr. Belson! We exchanged hellos.

Our table was down in front. After drinks and dinner, the show began. It was great. Bennett was in full voice, and Belson was a mad drummer with his solos. Bennett finished the show with his signature "I Left My Heart in San Francisco." Very cool. The ladies were impressed.

When the show was over, we hired a cab and took the girls back to their apartment, and said goodnight. Bruce and I decided to hit a pub nearby. Two hours later, and after more Australian beers, we staggered out, and started walking, we thought, back to our motel.

We stumbled down a main thoroughfare in Sydney's city center, drunk and lost. We were sitting in the middle of the thoroughfare when unexpectedly, a taxi pulled up. The cab driver got out and told us to get into the back seat, which we did. He closed the cab door and started to drive away.

"Where ya headin', Mates?" he asked. I couldn't remember where our motel was, so I took out my room key and showed him.

"Bloody Hell," he said, "you blokes are really pissed [drunk], and your bed sit [apartment] is cooee [far away]. No worries, I'll get you home." We sat, grinning stupidly as he turned the cab around, and headed back to where our motel was. About ten minutes later, we were there.

He stopped the cab, turned around to us and said, "You Yanks aren't used to our grog [beer]. It's strong, full of alcohol. Watch it. The coppers would toss you into the nick [jail] if they saw you like this. Go get some sleep." He got out and opened the cab door for us. I reached into my pocket to pay him, and he held up his hand.

"Not bloody likely, Mate." We got out of the cab, and staggered to our room.

The next morning, I woke up on my bed with my clothes on, and Bruce was on the floor, still dressed, sleeping. I gently woke him, and we looked at each other for a minute. Then we realized we were supposed to take the girls to the Sydney Zoo, so we got out of our clothes, cleaned up and shaved, put on some casual clothes and headed out to meet them.

We told them about the cab driver, and they both agreed that we were lucky he got to us because the Sydney police were tough on drunk GIs, and the fines were very high. As Margaret, my R&R girl said, "That bloke was fair dinkum [the cabbie was a good guy]." We agreed.

Bruce and I were very careful with Australian grog the rest of the week. We saw all the great sites in Sydney: the famous bridge, the new Opera House almost completed, the Botanical Gardens. We took the ferry to the Sydney Zoo, across the harbor from Circular Quay, and generally had a wonderful week. When our leave ended, Bruce and I said farewell to the ladies, and gave them the rest of our Australian money for their dry cleaning, then returned to the R&R center, signed in, turned in the civilian clothes. We put our jungle fatigues on, boarded the Boeing 707,

the sweet taste of normal life that week turning sour as we flew
back to Vietnam.

CHAPTER 24

Communion

I first met Ahn when I arrived at my duty post at Long Binh back in September of 1969. I was making myself at home in my new living quarters, the wooden hooch I was going to call home for the next twelve months. The hooch, a two-story barracks structure, was built without walls, just slats covered with screens to provide circulation in the hot climate. Each floor was divided into "bays" with low wooden partitions.

I taped a photo of my girlfriend on the wall locker, tacked a Peace poster ("War is not healthy for children and other living things") over the bunk, and hung a set of rosary beads, given to me by my dad when I left for the war, on the bunk frame. I was sweat-soaked from the hot sun, so I changed into a dry set of fatigues.

I just finished buttoning my shirt when a woman entered the hooch bay sweeping the floor around the bunks. She used a short-handled broom made of straw. She was one of the local women hired as a "hooch maid" to clean the barracks, and do the soldier's laundry.

She stopped sweeping when she saw my rosary hanging off the bunk. Pointing to it she looked at me and said, "Catholic?" I nodded, yes, a bit surprised she spoke English.

"I am Catholic too," she said. "My name is Ahn, like Saint Ahn."

She smiled.

I smiled back at her and said, "My name is Tom, like St. Thomas."

She was the first Vietnamese person since my arrival in country that didn't scowl at me. Most Vietnamese called us crazy (điên đầu) or assholes (lo dit) and GIs called them dinks, gooks, or slopes.

Ahn was a tiny woman, about 4 feet 7 inches tall, and very thin. She was nineteen or twenty years old and dressed in the uniform of hooch maids, loose silk black pants and a white long-sleeved shirt, and sandals. She wore a silver colored cross on a chain around her neck. I became friends with her, thanks to those rosary beads and our religion, even though I'd put my faith away during my time in the Army. I had seen too much meanness, cruelty and corruption. I rarely prayed or even thought about God or the Church. Then Ahn stirred it up again.

Whenever Ahn saw me in the barracks, she would ask me what saint's feast day it was, to see if I went to Mass. Of course, I never knew, and she chided me for that, which I took graciously and promised to do better. Our headquarters chaplain usually held an outdoor Sunday Mass and Holy Day Masses up in the parking area of the headquarters, but I was either working or, if I had time off, back in the hooch drinking beer with the guys.

One day Ahn gave me a small colored card, with the prayer to St. Anne on one side, in Vietnamese, and a depiction of the saint and the Virgin Mary, on the other. Both figures had Vietnamese facial features and wore áo dais, the traditional dress of upper-class Vietnamese women.

"She keep you safe," Ahn said, and told me to "put in pocket." I put the card in my wallet. We did not talk about politics, or the war. She spoke about her husband, who had been a farmer before the Army, and her children. I told her about my family back home.

Ahn told me that her family fled the North when the former Indochina was partitioned into North and South Vietnam in 1954. Many Catholics there were afraid of the Communist government in North Vietnam, and fled to the south, which declared itself a democracy. She had two children, and her husband was in the South Vietnamese Army, fighting somewhere with the Americans. She had not seen or heard from him in a year.

Anh one day asked me about my girlfriend's photo on the locker. I told her that her name was Kathleen, and that she was a *giao vien*, a teacher in America. Impressed, Ahn also asked if she were my *người yêu*, my sweetheart. I said yes, she was. Ahn, ever the defender of the Roman Catholic Faith, then asked if my sweetheart was *cong giao*, a Catholic. I said, yes again, and Ahn was pleased.

Ahn and her partner Ut, who was a Buddhist and hooch maid, worked in the barrack together. Ut was very shy and let Ahn do all the talking to us soldiers. The women had to check into the base in the morning, and were escorted out in the afternoon. Ahn and her partner would lift laundry bags, five or six at a time, and walk up and down the wooden stairs to the company laundry and shower stalls.

They worked in my company area hooches, staying together during the work day as protection from guys who thought they were good time girls (prostitutes). Some maids were also prostitutes but Ahn and Ut did not associate with them.

These maids needed all the money they could earn for their families. The company they worked for paid them about 10 MPC a month, so I paid them with a carton of Newport or Salem cigarettes each month off my Army ration card. These cigarette brands were menthol flavored, and popular among the Vietnamese. Black-market operators paid the women good money for them.

At Christmas 1969, we exchanged Christmas cards. I gave her one that had Santa in his red suit riding on a sleigh in snow. She gave me a holy card, of course. It depicted the Virgin and child and in Vietnamese *"Giáng Sinh vui ve"* (Merry Christmas). I still have it.

In August I received my orders to leave Vietnam on September 5, 1970. I told Ahn I was due to leave in three weeks. She invited me to have a farewell lunch with her and Ut. It is a very significant in Vietnamese culture to be invited to share a meal, let alone eat with a lowly American soldier. Ahn told me that other hooch maids didn't like the idea of our lunch. My GI buddies and co-workers had reservations, too.

"Eating with the gooks and eating their food! That's weird, man," one GI told me. Another cautioned me that "they might be Viet Cong" and poison me. I ignored them.

Knowing that it was a special occasion, I came down to lunch in my cleanest fatigues and cap. I brought more cigarettes, wrapped in the customary red tissue paper for gifts, and a surprise gift for Ahn. They graciously accepted the cigarettes and led me to an area near the open shower stalls, where most of the Vietnamese ate their lunch.

Ut ignited a little Primus gas stove and quickly there was a pot of water steaming away. A large woven reed mat was on the ground next to the stove, and smaller pots with vegetables, bean sprouts, leafy greens, chili peppers, pieces of chicken, and fat noodles were all arranged.

Ut waved a fan to keep the flies off the food. Ahn opened a bottle of Vietnamese beer, Ba Muoi Ba (33 beer), and presented it to me.

All the ingredients danced in the pot for a few minutes, then Ut handed Ahn two bowls, and Ahn quickly placed noodles and chicken in both, then ladled the broth in, piled the veggies and sprouts on top. She handed Ut a bowl, who passed it to me, and did the same again for Ut. Then she made one for herself and passed out the chopsticks.

This was my first time eating pho, and I was very clumsy trying to use the chopsticks. The noodles, chicken and veggies kept falling off them. The ladies giggled at my attempts to eat, till Ahn handed me one of the large spoons. The broth was spicy from the peppers and I cooled my burning throat with the Ba Muoi Ba. The heat of the chilis didn't bother the ladies.

Ahn and I made small talk, and she told me about the food, especially the chilis which were hot and came from a farm in the village near the base. I talked about my family and where I lived in America and what snow was. Ut listened, but said nothing. We finished the pho and I drank the last of my beer. It was time for me to get back to the headquarters compound. I stood up to say goodbye.

Ut clasped her hands together and bowed her head in thanks. Ahn took my hand in hers and said, "You are nice GI. You go home, go to Mass." She smiled at the joke.

I clasped her hands, and surprised her with my special gift— my father's rosary beads. Surprised, she bowed in thanks and said, "*Cam on*" (thank you).

I folded my hands and said in my horrible accent, "*Tam Biet*" (goodbye), then headed back to my job the headquarters area.

I saw Ahn once more just before I left. She was across the dirt street from me, coming out of another hooch carrying two laundry bags, doing what she did for me all year. I waved to her and she waved back.

I was glad to be leaving, going back to my life at home, but was sad that this hard-working, good-hearted woman lived such a hard life. I wondered if my friend would find another Catholic soldier to invite to lunch. Two days later, I boarded the plane that would take me back home.

CHAPTER 25

DEROS Day

September 5th, 1970. That was my DEROS, the military term for Date Estimated Return from Overseas (DEROS) to begin out-processing from Vietnam. My original date was October 25th, but President Nixon was pulling US troops out of the war at a rapid pace, so I caught a break. During my tour in Vietnam, Nixon invaded Cambodia, and men had gone to the Moon. The Mets won a World Series, the Bruins a Stanley Cup. College students celebrated Earth Day and students protested the war on Moratorium Day. Women marched and burned their bras in protest for equal rights. And the war became "Vietnamized" as more US combat operations were turned over to the Republic of Vietnam Army (ARVN).

It was a short jeep ride to the 90th Replacement Center on September 4. Most of my personal effects had been shipped home two weeks earlier. All I had left entering the out-processing center was a duffel bag full of clothes and odds and ends. Two hundred other soldiers with the same DEROS date arrived there too.

The guys most anxious to leave were the combat veterans, many just back from jungle bases. Heavily tanned and skinny, almost gaunt, many wore dirty, faded and torn fatigues. They had long hair and were nervously looking around at the buildings, the barracks of "Disneyland East" seeing things they hadn't seen for months, like shower stalls, toilets, barracks.

An announcement over the PA system called us to a formation. A master sergeant wearing the bright green jungle fatigues of a newly arrived soldier ("newbie") said he was going to pull an inspection on us. We looked at each other? Inspection? He walked up and down the formation, telling guys to "shine those boots," "get a haircut," asking "where's your dog tags," and other basic training shit like that.

When he finished inspecting, he explained: "The Army don't want you bastards getting off that Boeing freedom bird in the US looking like you just came out of the jungle (though it was clear some WERE just out of the jungle). Clean up, shave, get your hair cut, put on fresh fatigues. If I see anyone not looking sharp, I'm not gonna let him board that plane, understand?"

We were angry. We wondered who the fuck is this guy? Keep us off our trip home? No way! But we wanted to get on that plane, and so we cleaned up. GIs angrily opened their duffels for a change of fatigues. Guys shaved in the latrine area, while some took open showers wearing their fatigues and nylon jungle boots to clean them. The heat of the day would dry them off quickly. A Vietnamese barber was doing land office business cutting hair.

Later that day, we stood in a line as the Army re-checked our DEROS orders and inspected our duffel bags for weapons and drugs. I ate dinner in the same goddam mess hall I ate in last year when I arrived in country, and planned to just hang around waiting for morning to board the plane, or freedom bird.

When night came, I was edgy. They gave me a bunk, but no mattress. Didn't matter, I couldn't sleep. Nighttime in Vietnam was dangerous. The enemy fired rockets at the big base at night.

I was too close to getting home to have a rocket attack stop me from leaving. Flares went up from the artillery teams out to the edge of the Post, lighting the perimeter and firing H&I rounds (harassment and interdiction) out into the countryside.

Gunships flew low over the rice paddies outside the perimeter, spraying red fire from their mini-guns. Green fire from the enemy reached the sky trying to shoot them down. I stayed awake all night.

The next morning, September 5th, my date to leave, I formed up again with the others, all of us in "clean" fatigues and boots and with new haircuts. We waited for the Sergeant to call our names to go home. When he came out and called formation, there was a Captain next to him, and he stepped forward and addressed us.

"Men, there has been a change in orders. Your plane has been requisitioned by the Military Police to transfer US military personnel who committed crimes while in country back to the United States for prosecution. You all will have to wait another day for your freedom bird. As our Vietnamese friends say, "*XIN LOI!*" (which loosely meant in English— SORRY ABOUT THAT!). That is all. Sergeant, dismiss the men." He quickly turned and left.

Another Day! So close to leaving and now this shit! Loud curses flew out of the formation. Soldiers were stomping around swearing. Like the other soldiers, I was so anxious to go home on that day, full of expectations, and now this Captain yanked it all away.

I stayed in the departure barracks the rest of the day, anxious and angry. My experience in the Army taught me that any change in the routine could be dangerous. I just wanted to get the hell out of there. I spent a second sleepless night in DEROS hell. That night, the flares, the mini-guns, and the artillery once again did their deadly work while I stayed awake.

The next morning, September 6th, at 8:00 AM, after a quick breakfast, the Sergeant called another roll call formation. We stood there waiting to hear about more delays, but the Sergeant told us we had five minutes to "get our shit together" to board buses to the flight line at Bien Hoa Air Base, for our freedom bird. A cheer went up. I quickly gathered my duffel, and boarded one of the waiting olive-green colored buses. When full, the buses headed over to Bien Hoa Air Base nearby.

The trip took about fifteen minutes. I don't remember much about the ride. At the air terminal, I could see my plane taxiing to a stop. It was a Boeing 707, with "Flying Tiger Air" painted on its side. It came to a stop. Somebody rolled the stairway up to the plane, the door opened and soldiers dressed in brand new jungle fatigues came out of the plane.

My group hooted and hollered at them to hurry up and get out of our plane. They walked by us. Shouts of "You'll be so-r-r-r-y—It's a long year for you, FNG!" (fucking new guy)— escorted the new arrivals into the terminal. I had heard those same taunts last year when I came in country. It didn't take long to board the plane, and when the pretty flight attendants closed the doors, the plane taxied away from the terminal.

Everyone held their breath. The plane lifted off, and loud cheers drowned out the noise of the engines. My DEROS had begun for real. The flight route was Tokyo, Japan, Anchorage, Alaska, then Travis Air Force Base, California. I was going home, to my family, Kathy and the beginning of a new life, finally.

CHAPTER 26

Coming Home

The flight landed at Travis Air Force Base, just outside Fairfield, California. All of us were bused to Oakland Army Base. We drove on Route 80 through Vallejo, San Pablo and Berkeley, towns and cities I never visited before. Staring out the window as we drove along, I watched all the traffic and people going about their business, driving their delivery trucks, riding their motorcycles, shopping, walking. There were no sandbag bunkers, the hills were brown, not jungle green, there was no barbed wire, no men with weapons. The stench and heat were missing. There was no war in California, USA.

Out-processing included a physical exam, a psychiatric exam, the return of jungle issue for stateside fatigues, and then a steak dinner, compliments of President Nixon. The meal was served to us by soldiers who were going to Vietnam the next morning.

I filled out more forms and travel documents, and since I was going to be discharged from the Army, and was to travel on the Army ticket, I had to wear the uniform they issue you when you are formally discharged. I was measured for my olive-green dress uniform, with all my ribbons, rank and unit patches. The last of the forms were stamped, the cashier counted out my last GI pay, and I was handed a thank you form letter from President Nixon for my service to the nation. I was officially discharged. It only took twenty-four hours.

Wearing my new Class A uniform, I hailed a cab outside the base and headed for San Francisco International Airport. It was 5:00 AM, almost a day since I arrived in the United States. I looked for a pay phone to call my girl Kathy back in Boston. There was a bank of pay telephone booths located in the middle of the corridor. I put in a dime and nickel from my pocket and dialed the operator. I explained that that I just returned from Vietnam and had no more change and asked her to call Kathy's number, collect, in Boston. I knew she would be just getting up and ready for work, I wanted to tell her I was on my way.

The operator placed the call and when Kathy picked up, her voice was full of surprise, and happiness. I was happy to hear her voice, too. I gave her my flight number and arrival time, and she said she'd meet me at Logan Airport in Boston. When the call finished, the operator came on and said to hang up. I did, and the phone discharged nickels and dimes from the coin box. The phone rang again and I picked up. The operator said, "Here's some change in case you need to make more calls, soldier," then hung up.

There must have been five dollars' worth of change in the coin box. I put it all in my pocket. I looked around. The place was deserted. The long concourse with ticket counters on each side was empty, the counters closed. I didn't know what to do. A Redcap luggage porter, wearing a red cap and dark blue shirt and pants, appeared from a door behind the United Airlines counter.

"Hey, soldier! You hungry?" he shouted.

"Yeah, but there's no place open," I replied.

He smiled and said, "Follow me, we'll git you some food."

Hitching my duffel higher on my shoulder and with my small travel bag in my hand, I followed him through the door labelled "Authorized Personnel Only." After going down some stairs, we turned a corner into a garage area under the main concourse.

A small café was tucked inside the garage, along a wall. There were four stools along a counter, and a small flattop grill and stove against the wall. The white plastic menu above the grill listed items and prices in red stick-on letters. A large fluorescent light fixture above the grill cast a cool light over the café. The garage smelled of oil and gasoline.

A large black woman was cooking on the grill. She wore a pink waitress outfit, complete with little cap and a white apron. A man wearing overalls with "United" printed on the back was sitting on a stool and sipping coffee. Redcap and I joined him.

"Mama, this boy is hungry," said the Redcap, "what can you do for him?"

Mama turned, smiled at me and said, "Honey, what would you like?"

I thought for a second or two, and said "Ham and eggs sunny side, and toast, if that's okay." After the long trip and the busy discharge process, and the steak dinner I barely touched, I was hungry.

"What kind of toast, honey?"

"Gee, raisin bread if you got it." I hadn't had raisin bread toast for a long time.

"Sure do, sit yourself down." I sat next to the United man.

He asked me, "What you doin' here so early, you goin' on leave?"

"No, sir. I just got out of the Army and I'm going home."

He nodded. "Was you overseas?"

"Yeah, Vietnam."

Mama put a steaming cup of coffee in front of me and made a sad sound like tsk.

"Vietnam?" he said. "My cousin's boy never did come back from there. Was a Marine. Got it up at Khe Sanh, you know? His mama is still grieving, two years later." I nodded but said nothing. I poured real cream in my coffee, and added sugar. My Redcap friend joined in.

"I was in Korea, that hell hole, freezing my ass off, was an Army trucker. Came back and nobody gave a damn about me coming home 'cept my kin. Them boys who beat the Germans and the Japs, they got parades and shit. I got nothin." He held up his coffee mug.

"Mama, can you give me a refill?" he said. Then he looked at me. I sipped the hot liquid in my cup. It was a strong brew. "You went through some shit there, too, right?" I nodded, no use telling him about the mortars and rockets, the fear, the heat, the snipers.

"Well, you won't git nothing for it, neither," he said. He jerked his head to make his point, then drank some more of his coffee. The United man looked at me and said, "I'll bet your Mama is happy."

"I haven't called home yet," I said. "But she knows I'm on my way."

Mama turned from the griddle and said, "Here's your breakfast, honey." She put a plate in front of me with three perfectly fried eggs, two thick slices of ham and the toast. "Eat up. You look like they don't feed you over there. I'll git you some more coffee," and she turned to the Cory coffee station. The United guy snickered.

"Hell, Mama, that Army don't care to feed them boys right. They give em cans of beans and Spam to eat, right? Jest' wanna put em in that shit and hope they doan get their asses shot."

"Don't you use that language in my place, Jeremy." She frowned. "This boy just got back from a bad place, and you just let him alone so he can eat." She smiled at me. "Now you eat that, honey," and she poured more coffee in my cup.

Redcap asked, "Where you heading, soldier?"

"Boston, Massachusetts," I said. "My girlfriend Kathy lives just outside the city. She's a schoolteacher." Mama smiled when she heard that.

"She wrote me almost every day while I was over there. I got most of the letters, but the mail screwed up a lot." I bit into the raisin toast. It was delicious.

"Never been East, never been. Too cold for me," said Redcap. "How about you Jeremy? Been to Boston?"

"No, can't say I ever was. Got to New York City once but didn't stay long. Too crowded. I took the train back here licketty split." Looking serious, Jeremy turned to me and said, "You maybe should get out of that uniform and wear something else whilst you travel."

"Why?" I asked.

"Well, we got college kids coming to the airport now, protestin' this war, and now they're right pissed off about that story of those Vietnamese villagers what got shot last week. The newspaper is calling it a massacre."

I remembered that. It happened just before I left. The village was full of enemy fighters using civilians as shields, but some captain had artillery blow the place to hell, anyway. He and his lieutenants were charged with killing civilians when they got back to their base camp.

Jeremy continued, "Folks are upset about it. There's been some fistfights with GIs in uniform like yourself here at the airport." That upset me. They told us at Oakland about protesters, but most of us didn't pay attention.

"They come at me, no big deal. I can handle those guys. Anyway, I'm travelling on Army tickets, so I have to wear the uniform." I stabbed at my ham, angry at the thought of trouble on my way home.

"Suit yourself son, just watch out. Don't git yourself in trouble. Them MPs will drag you to jail if you mess with them kids. If they bother you, smile. Like what Dr. King said, "Resist violence with Love, or something like that.""

The two men finished their coffee and got up, put some money on the counter, and left. "You take care," Jeremy said as he left. Redcap just nodded goodbye.

Mama said, "You finish up all of it, now. I got to wash some dishes. Be back shortly." She went through the door into the back room. I ate the last of the ham and eggs and drained my cup of coffee. I stood and was reaching for my wallet to pay when Mama came back out.

"No sir! No! You put that back! We all proud of you, don't pay no mind to those protesters. Now you go back upstairs, they be opening the counters any minute, and you get yourself home, honey."

"Yes, ma'am," I mumbled. "Thank you."

I went back up the stairs, and sure enough, the counters were opening. It was 6:30 AM. People were trickling into the concourse, cabs were pulling up, and it was getting busy. I noticed the young women, the "round-eyed girls" as we called them in Vietnam. I saw very few of them in country.

The women I was used to seeing daily were Vietnamese women. These round-eyed women were all sizes and shapes and colors and they all looked great in their mini-skirts.

I got my one-way ticket stamped to Boston, and baggage-checked my duffel. The flight was due to leave in sixty minutes, so I called home, and my brother Dan answered.

It was 9:30 AM back home. "Holy shit, Tom, where are you?" he asked.

"I'm in San Francisco, about to fly out this morning—be in Boston to see Kathy in five or six hours. Tell the folks."

"You got it, man," he said, and hung up.

As I walked back toward the ticket counter and gate, I saw a group of young people carrying anti-war signs coming down the wide concourse. They spotted my uniform and headed toward me.

One of them, a tall, slim guy with long blond hair, wearing jeans and a t-shirt, came up close, his eyes bright. My stomach tightened.

"Hey GI, how many babies you kill over there?" he said. The others came over and joined him. They all seemed high, their eyes bright, their pupils wide open, and they had goofy smiles on their faces.

I had seen that look on GIs who smoked a lot of pot, "Cambodian Gold" we called it. I said nothing and started to walk past them.

He shouted at me as I passed, "Fucking baby killer!"

My face got red and I was embarrassed, but I just smiled at them like Jeremy said, and I kept walking. I turned in my Army ticket, and when my flight was called, I boarded and was directed to the last seat in the plane. Absolutely the ass end of the half-empty 707. So much for travel with Army tickets.

I put my uniform cap and small travel bag in the overhead bin, unbuttoned my dress uniform jacket, and sat down. The seat belt light went on, and I fastened mine. The engines started, and the plane pushed off, taxied, and then lifted into the air. I was more excited by this flight than the one that I took out of Vietnam. I was really going back to Boston and Kathy. I was going to have a normal life again.

A tall, shapely flight attendant with flowing red hair came down the aisle, checking to see if people had their seat belts fastened, and stopped at my seat. She reminded me of the actress Maureen O'Hara, with her crimson locks, clear blue eyes and smiling face. I smiled in return. She looked at my jacket, with my stripes and ribbons.

"Going home, Specialist?" she asked.

"Yes, ma'am," I said. "Back to Boston."

"Call me Annie." She looked at my ribbons again, and frowned, "Vietnam?"

"Yes," I said.

"Well, you relax." Her smile returned.

"Can I get you anything for breakfast?" I was tired, been up for 24 hours. I needed a shower and sleep. And those college kids pissed me off. So, I joked, "Yeah, I'd love an Irish coffee, Annie."

She smiled at me and said, "Coming right up!"

The plane reached its cruising altitude and leveled off. I heard the food trolley being set up. Then I saw Annie coming down the aisle carrying a small tray with a cup, sugar, cream and a small steel carafe of coffee. She put my seat tray down and placed the coffee on it.

"As ordered," she said. She gave a furtive glance over her shoulder, then with a cat's smile, pulled two small bottles of Johnny Walker Whiskey from her apron pocket and placed them on the tray.

"Welcome home, Specialist," she said. She turned back up the aisle to serve the other passengers. I poured one whiskey into the cup, added coffee, cream and sugar, drank it and repeated till I had finished two cups of Irish coffee.

Annie came back a little later and took the cup, cream and the empty bottles off my seat tray. The coffee and whiskey made me sleepy. I'd made it back "to the world" in one piece. Two years of Army life, a life of anger, fear, hate and violence and war were finished for me. My homecoming so far was great; a free breakfast, free whiskey, and change in my pocket. The protesters couldn't put a dent in my contentment. I was going home, home to Kathy ready for whatever came next for us. I put my head back and slept all the way to Boston.

Epilogue

I went back to where it began. It was September of 1970, four days after coming back from Vietnam. I returned to the seminary south of Boston where I spent five and one-half years living in a religious community.

I parked my rental and walked up to the front door of the seminary wearing my new Army Class A uniform, my rank on my sleeve, and my Vietnam Service and Campaign ribbons pinned over the left breast pocket of my green uniform jacket. I rang the doorbell. No one answered.

I rang the bell again to no response, so I tried the door. It was unlocked. I went in. I turned and faced the chapel. I thought about this place often when I was in the Army, and especially in Vietnam when huddled in a damp bunker during rocket attacks. It was a refuge for my stress and fear.

The chapel doors, hand carved bas-relief wood sculptures, were twelve feet high, and depicted colored images of Mary, Joseph and the Child Jesus. Joseph held in his hand a model of the seminary building. I opened the chapel doors and went in. The odor of candle wax in the air told me I had missed the morning mass. The simple granite altar that I served on many times as an altar assistant was bathed in the late morning light coming from the windows of the bell tower. Being in the chapel brought back the memory of how the old priests said their masses in Latin, the young ones defiantly in English.

140

I remember vowing to never say a Latin Mass when I became a priest.

I left the chapel, walked by the small garden in the foyer where the community of seminarians would gather each night after dinner to chant "Salve Regina," a Latin hymn, in front of the statue of the Virgin Mary that was placed in the garden. The garden was empty now, the statue gone. No one was in the halls, or in the office area where Father Superior changed my life two years ago.

Strolling down the hall with the chapel on one side, the courtyard on the other, I saw a large pile of dog excrement in the middle of the hall. It was shocking because I used to wax and polish that corridor every Saturday when I lived here. Woe be me then if I ever missed a spot to polish. Now, apparently, some priest owned a dog and the hall was its bathroom.

I turned back to office area to leave, and bumped into Father Brown, who was the new head of the seminary. He had been my Ethics teacher at the nearby college we seminarians attended. He was wearing slacks and a polo shirt, not a cassock and collar.

"Hi, Father," I said. He didn't recognize me at first. I'm sure it was my uniform, then it came to him who I was.

"Oh, it's you, Tom!" he said. "Glad to see you! So happy you came back. What brings you here?" We shook hands.

"I just wanted to visit the old place, Father. I just came back from Vietnam and wanted to see this place again," I said.

"Oh," he replied, "I didn't know you were over there. Are you okay?"

"Yes, Father. I'm okay. I was in a support unit. I did have some bad times, but I didn't kill anyone."

"Oh, good, God blessed you!" he said smiling. Jesus! I thought. Blessed me? I couldn't share with him my war: the bad times, my pneumonia, my struggle with the Army "Treatment" when I applied for conscience objector status. My loss of faith in the Church. The heat, the fear, rockets, sapper attacks, getting shot at by an old man in Vietnam. How could I tell him that the past two years were hell because his predecessor determined I had a temporary vocation?

"I'm holding down the fort and looking for my dog," he continued speaking. I laughed.

"I know where he has been, and he left you a gift." I pointed down the hall.

"Damn!" He swore. "I better clean it up before the janitor sees it."

"Janitor? I asked. "No postulants to clean it up?"

"No, Tom, we don't have many joining the seminary now. We may have to give this whole building to the college." I was shocked. My freshman class of seminarians had twenty-seven members seven years ago, and now there were none. What happened to the Church in such a short time?

"Well," I said, looking at my watch, "I have to go. Good to

see you Father, say hi to everyone." We shook hands again. I walked toward the front door while he scurried to clean up the dog's mess. I sat in my rented car for a minute and thought.

So many changes in two years, to my life, and to the seminary, the world, the Church and the religious community I had lived in for years. I was shocked how much life had changed during those years, especially the Church. Old rules were discarded, new theology and ideas about what it means to be a priest were changing the old, strict Latin-speaking religion.

When I was huddled in a damp, rat-infested bunker, hoping the Viet Cong didn't attack, I prayed to be back in that world of "God is love, blessed are the peacemakers, peace be with you," and all that. Watching machine guns spraying red tracer fire out into the paddies, the green enemy tracer fire replying, seeing the enemy bodies on the wire, I knew I could never return to that world, not after Vietnam.

The world that Father lived in, one of order, Latin masses, strict obedience to a hierarchy, Gregorian Chants, celibacy, black cassocks and clerical collars, a world he treasured and tried to protect wasn't going to return. That world had collapsed.

I started the rental car and drove away to begin another life.

The author in the seminary.

Ahn, the housekeeper, the author's
Catholic friend in Vietnam.

The author at Long Binh next to his jeep.

Acknowledgements

As I write this it has been 50 years since these events in my life occurred. My memory of these events has been with me every day. Some details are sharper than others, some are less sharp, but my emotions are depicted accurately.

The two years I spent in the US Army from 1968 to 1970 were in sharp contrast to the five-plus years I spent studying to be a priest and living a religious life in a Roman Catholic Seminary in Massachusetts. This book is a record of my struggle to find my way from living a holy life to a life of combat.

Names of people have been changed in some cases, but the places have not. Some of the events depicted I have had to render from memory, and thanks to my own journal, plus letters and photographs saved by my dear wife, helped me in reconstructing the events I described.

I would like to thank Matthew Brennan, a Vietnam Veteran and excellent writer, for his inspiration and encouragements. Matt has written his two excellent books recounting his Vietnam war and its effect on him as he returned to civilian life.

I want to also thank Sean Davis, an Iraqi war veteran and writer, who encouraged me to write my memoir when I attended his nonfiction workshop at the William Joiner Institute's Writers' Workshop at the University of Massachusetts, Boston.

I want to thank Roxana Von Kraus, my writing instructor at the AGAPE Writing Workshops for Veterans which I attended at Woods College, Boston College in 2018. Roxana provided me with encouragement to pursue completing this memoir.

My thanks to my editor, Catherine Parnell, who is a real professional and knows how to make a writer better, and to my book designer, Christa Johnson, for such a lovely job.

Finally, my thanks and love to my wife Kathleen for her encouragement and patience, and her assistance in making this book happen.

About The Author

Tom Keating entered the Holy Cross Seminary in North Easton, Massachusetts just after high school, and he lived a semi-monastic religious life for over five years. After leaving the seminary, Tom enlisted and served in the United States Army in 1968, and served one year in Long Binh in the Republic of Vietnam, from 1969 to 1970. His work there earned him two Army Commendation medals.

Honorably discharged, Tom attended Boston University and completed his Master's degree in Education, and taught high school media studies in Burlington, Massachusetts for eight years. A career in corporate media communications followed.

Tom attended the writing program for veterans at the Woods College of Advancing Studies at Boston College under the direction of Roxana Von Kraus, and was twice accepted at the Joiner Institute Writers' Workshop at the University of Massachusetts, Boston. His story "Convoy for the Con Voi" was published in *War Stories 2017*, an anthology edited by Sean Davis. Tom's story "Shakedown" appears in *Complacency Kills*.

Tom and his wife live in Needham, Massachusetts. He is an active member of the Veterans of Foreign Wars, Post 2498, Needham and is committed to assisting veterans of all ages.

Made in the USA
Middletown, DE
07 January 2020

82729065R00104